A 31-Day Adventure into the Heart of God's Great Love

Bridging THE *Gap*

Audacious Love

Audacious Love: A 31-Day Adventure into the Heart of God's Great Love

Copyright © 2017 | Bridging the Gap

ISBN-13: 978-1976334443 (Print)

Publishing and Design Services | MartinPublishingServices.com

Contents

SECTION 3: AUDACIOUS LOVE INSPIRES ME TO...

Introduction

Words.

Audacious: daring, bold, fearless, brave, reckless, courageous, heroic, valiant, daredevil, venturesome, gutsy, spunky, confident, shocking, surprising, unconventional, intrepid.

As you can probably tell, I am very passionate about the word *audacious*.

To me, this word is a descriptor of the extreme love God has for me and for all of us—his children. He calls our names gently and pursues our hearts tenaciously, and because his love is unconditional, he will never, ever stop.

His pursuit is relentless and oftentimes unconventional. I know this to be true for me. And while he chooses to reveal himself in countless, personal ways each day, the most audacious example of all was the choice to send his only son, Jesus, to die for the sins of the world.

His Word says that God sacrificed his only Son on our behalf so that each of us could choose to have eternal life through him. I am often overwhelmed by this valiant act of courage. It is my heart's desire that you would have the opportunity to get to know this fearless Jesus as your Savior, as well as your best friend—one who will never leave you or forsake you.

As Jesus gave and continues to give his all for us, **I believe his desire is that we, too, would audaciously love him with all of our heart and audaciously love others with all of our heart.** I believe he wants each of us to be his extension, or "hands and feet," of love to the world around us—beginning at home, with our families.

Acts 1:8 says, "…and you will be my witnesses in Jerusalem, and in all Judea and Samaria, and to the ends of the earth."

My simple prayer is this: that you would become relentless in your pursuit of knowing him and that you would be so confident in your relationship with him that his audacious love would organically spill out and over into your home, community, nation, and world!

Much Love,

Carol Lund
Director, Bridging the Gap

1

Audacious Love

Reassuring

Lysa TerKeurst

"Whatever is true … think about such things …
And the God of peace will be with you."

Philippians 4:8b, 9b (NIV)

If you've ever heard me give my testimony, you know part of what I share is being a little girl twirling around next to my daddy, wishing I could know that he loved me.

Maybe in his own way, he did love me. But something was broken in our relationship that left me feeling desperate for reassurance.

Over the years, God has healed my heart in miraculous ways. Through God's promises I've been reassured of all those things I wished my earthly father would have said. I know God's love for me is deep, unwavering, and certain.

But there are still times I catch myself twirling again. Crying out again. Wishing I could feel totally secure. Hating my insecurities. And mad that this struggle I thought was over, surfaces still.

Maybe it always will.

And maybe that's not such a bad thing.

For it keeps me desperate for a reassurance I can't get any other way. It keeps me desperate for God.

I can stand in an arena with thousands of people clapping for the message I just gave ... and still feel my heart desperately twirling.

I can conquer my food demons and finally fit back into my skinny jeans ... and still feel my heart desperately twirling.

The only thing that stops the desperation, the uncertainties, the insecurities, the twirling ... is for the Spirit of God to lay across my heart and make it still. The blanket of his presence and his protection is the only perfect fit for the deep creases and crevices carved inside me.

I don't know what tough things you've been through, sweet sister, but I do know this: *Brokenness is universal.* We all have things in life that trigger deep insecurities and our own personal "twirling about," searching for reassurance.

But here's the amazing thing.

While brokenness is universal, God's redemption is also universal for those who proclaim Christ as Lord. No matter what cracks and crevices we have in our hearts, if we seek the truth of God above all else, he is enough to fill in those raw places.

"Whatever is true ... think about such things ...
And the God of peace will be with you."

Philippians 4:8b, 9b

Have you caught your heart twirling, desperate for reassurance lately? Today, spend a few minutes letting these truths fill your mind and seep into those desperate places of your heart:

"The LORD your God is with you,
the Mighty Warrior who saves. He will take great delight in
you; in his love he will no longer rebuke you;
but will rejoice over you with singing."

Zephaniah 3:17, NIV

"I pray that you … may have power, together with all the Lord's holy people, to grasp how wide and long and high and deep is the love of Christ."

Ephesians 3:17b, 18, NIV

"Cast all your anxiety on him because he cares for you."

1 Peter 5:7, NIV

*"The LORD appeared to us in the past, saying:
'I have loved you with an everlasting love;
I have drawn you with unfailing kindness.'"*

Jeremiah 31:3, NIV

I pray these truths flood your heart with peace like they do mine. Peace that gives you permission to stop twirling and start to *live like you are loved.*

Because you are.

Deeply. Abundantly. And without end.

REFLECT AND RESPOND

What things trigger your heart to feel desperate? Choose one of the Scripture-based truths Lysa shared to meditate on, and memorize it this week.

Loneliness, Straying from God
1 Peter 5:7, NIV

Lysa TerKeurst is a *New York Times* bestselling author and president of Proverbs 31 Ministries. She lives in North Carolina with her family. Connect with her at www. LysaTerKeurst.com or on social media @LysaTerKeurst.

AUDACIOUS LOVE IS

Reckless

Renee Griffith

"And hope does not put us to shame, because God's love has been poured into our hearts through the Holy Spirit who has been given to us."

Romans 5:5 (NIV)

I stood in the doorway of my room, looking down the hallway at two crammed-full suitcases stacked at the top of the stairs. Their stressed zippers barely managed to contain all I would see of America for the next two years.

I was on my way to the Eastern European country of Moldova. The only problem was that I was several thousand dollars short on my budget, and I couldn't be given clearance to join the host missionaries until all money was raised. Okay, there was another problem too—my term was supposed to begin in five days.

As I stared at the stuffed suitcases, my mind shot back to a youth convention in Helena, Montana, when God spoke to my 12-year-old heart, asking if I would exchange my life goal (becoming an astronaut) for his plan for my life (becoming a missionary). After a night of tearful deliberation, I said yes and never looked back.

Fast forward ten years. There I stood, a freshly-minted college graduate ready to step into my calling. People in college knew me as the girl who was there to get enough intercultural studies training to move overseas. I had no plan B.

But five days before my slated take-off, I had a snowball's chance in a Georgian July of going to the land where God had called me. I nervously withheld making any plans for a going-away party *just in case* things didn't come through.

Oh, I knew God *could* get me there; he can do anything. I just didn't know if he *would*.

I grew up singing songs about God's illimitable greatness. I saw his strength as I watched him sustain my mom through two major surgeries. I heard his power as I listened to my dad lead my cousin to the Lord. I felt his care as I ran on a newly-straightened knee God divinely healed. But this one—this several-thousand dollar deficit based on a preteen dream…

God, I know you can. But will *you?*

I asked that question every single day that summer. And as I wrestled with my balance of belief and doubt, God revealed to me that our ability to exercise faith depends in large part on what we believe about the character of God and his abilities and intentions for us personally. I can quote Bible verses with the best of them, but unless I personalize the truths I hear, my heart remains locked to the purposes of God.

God is infinite. God is holy. God is truth. He is wisdom. He is mercy. He is grace.

And above all, God is love. First John 4:8 describes God in this way, and chapter 3 verse 16 of both John and 1 John give body to this re-name, explaining that to love is to lay down one's life for another.

When I'm praying to God out of a place of great need, I must first remember that I am praying to love personified.

Romans 8:32 puts it this way: "He who did not spare his own Son, but gave him up for us all—how will he not also, along with him, graciously give us all things?" If God showed us the ultimate act of love through the death of his son, why would we expect him to come up short in the other areas we need him—areas less crucial than salvation?

As I dwelled on the character of God—on his love—my fears and worries were assuaged. Yes, I faced a real time crunch, and no, I didn't have anything else lined up. But the goal of serving the people of Moldova I carried in my heart for a decade was more than just a wish. It was a hope, and "hope does not put us to shame, because God's love has been poured into our hearts through the Holy Spirit who has been given to us."

You see, when God gives us a dream and we hope in it, that hope won't embarrass us or fail us. *Not* because our hopes are always realistic but because the *love of God* is in us. Our God-given hopes are sustained and fulfilled *because God is love*. He has given us everything through the death and life of his son. Anything he calls us to can surely be fulfilled as we keep in step with him; Jesus is our guarantee.

***

Within an hour of stacking those stuffed suitcases at the top of the stairs, an acquaintance called and donated the amount of money I needed. My entrance into missions came as a last-minute abundance because the one who is love, the one who freely gave his son, graciously gives everything else we need.

That's pretty audacious if you ask me. And all that audacious love is pretty much the only thing that can make sense out of a two-suitcase trip around the world.

REFLECT AND RESPOND

What has God called you to—even years ago? Do you need to dust off that call?

_____

_____

_____

Remember the promise of Romans 5:5—that the love God has poured into your heart keeps your hope from turning into shame—and pray Romans 8:32 aloud as a reminder of the ultimate gift already credited to your account. God loves you audaciously, so a little recklessness in light of it may be the only proper response.

_____

_____

_____

Renee Griffith is a former missionary associate to Moldova and Russia and currently writes for AGWM's _WorldView_ magazine while finishing her M.Div. at the Assemblies of God Theological Seminary in Springfield, Missouri. In the free time she doesn't have, she enjoys playing classical piano and JustDancing.

Freeing

Lindsay May

*"Now the Lord is the Spirit, and where the
Spirit of the Lord is, there is freedom."*

2 Corinthians 3:17 (NIV)

For about a year, I felt trapped. I felt unexpectedly sorrowful and unsure of so many aspects of my life. Even while my husband and I celebrated the approach of our second child, my heart was mourning things I had unknowingly bound myself to. Despite the growing life in my womb, it was as though I was mourning a death. Things I thought God had desired for me I began to wrestle with: My purpose, relationships, career. I felt a deep rejection and wounding that I just couldn't shake.

"Lord, how could you allow this to happen to me? I thought you placed these good things in my life. If you're so good, why are you making me feel so much pain? Why am I never good enough?" These were the raw questions that I wrestled with almost daily. I knew in my head that God was good, but often wondered why I rarely felt like the beneficiary of his goodness. Somehow I thought I was not allowed to have good things in my life—that they were reserved for others. I believed I needed to keep my head down, be quiet, and fit in where others told me to be.

Deep down, I believed that God was all-powerful, but thought he surely must love others more than he loved me. There was no way he could use an average person like me.

The nine months of preparation for my son became a pregnancy within my spirit as I wrestled with the concept of God's goodness and his purpose for me. As the months progressed toward my due date, the Lord began to reveal how he viewed *me*. It was something he had given me a glimpse of as a child, but I had suppressed out of fear. In my vision, I was bold, confident, and secure, with a burning message for women to not settle for anything less than God's full and unique plan for each of them. Yet, I had spent so many years suppressing myself that I didn't think the things God was placing on my heart would fit how others viewed me—or how I *thought* they viewed me.

I thought that I'd just face more rejection if I began to take steps towards the things God was placing on my heart. Worse yet, I realized that I was waiting for someone to give me permission to try something new and recognize the strengths and abilities God placed in me. For a person whose love language is words of affirmation, letting go of what others weren't saying to me felt torturous, but God revealed to me that I was letting others write my story. Instead of being wrecked by the loneliness from the loss of deep friendships, I sought time with God and spoke his promises over my life. I began to focus on the things God entrusted me to steward: My husband, my daughter, the precious baby boy who was stretching my belly to the max, and my relationship with the Lord. Everything else I viewed as a luxury instead of what I was missing out on.

One cloudy morning as I was standing in my kitchen waiting for my daily (decaf) coffee to brew, I asked the Lord, "Will I ever feel such deep joy again?" Almost instantly, I heard the spirit whisper, "In my presence, there is fullness of joy, Lindsay." I decided that the only way to be totally free and healed from my own insecurities and deep wounds was to allow God's love to wash over me. To embrace the pain, press into it, and *choose* healing and freedom.

I began to do more of the only thing I could think to do—run to him. I ran to God for everything, confessing every negative thought and emotion as it came to me. The more time I spent running into the presence of God, the clearer my vision became. I began to see myself the way God saw me—free, wild, confident, and boldly lighting the hearts around me on fire with passion for the Lord. I learned to forgive others for things they didn't even realize had impacted me so deeply. Slowly my pain began to dissipate and was replaced with a new expectancy of hope. I finally believed that God had a good plan for *me*. In responding to God's goodness, I began to see the journey he was taking me on to untame my heart, to set me free through revealing the source of the pains and aches my spirit was going through.

The cold December night my son was born was a night of celebration. I celebrated a beautiful, healthy son, and also the birth of a new spirit in me. I often reflect in wonder at how God's audacious love for me allowed me to go through such deep emotional and spiritual valleys so that he could bring me such joy, hope, and freedom. A rebirth. What God did in the natural, he also did in the spirit. I am now free to love despite the pain I've experienced, and I have a new fire in my soul for wanting others to be free.

REFLECT AND RESPOND

Are you in the middle of a sorrowful situation? What outcome do you need to lay in God's hands to receive freedom? Are you choosing freedom or clinging to situations in your own strength?

_____

_____

_____

Lindsay May is a lifestyle photographer and entrepreneur with a mission to showcase the beauty of our world through her lens and writing at www.heartswild. com. She gets fired up about helping women fall in love with the Word and follow the calling God has placed on their lives, and holds a master's degree in Organizational Leadership. A mom to two little ones, Lindsay's days are filled with toddler-chasing and exploring the world from new perspectives.

Abundant

Anna Henke

*"How abundant are the good things that you have
stored up for those who fear you."*

Psalm 31:2 (NIV)

My dad has been in heaven for some years now, but when he was still with us one of his favorite things to do was give gifts. If you are familiar with *The Five Love Languages* by Gary Chapman, gift giving was definitely my dad's love language. Unsurprisingly, Christmas was his favorite time of the year! My family would go all out with a real tree, house décor, and, of course, presents—no one moreso than my dad.

Back in my childhood, my three sisters and I weren't allowed in the basement for the two-month period before Christmas. This was because it became what we affectionately deemed "dad's store." His tie drawer was a hiding place for small gifts like jewelry and scarves. His office was the resting place for bulkier items. Dad's philosophy was, *Buy it now and return it later, if necessary.*

You see, dad was so determined that we would all get the perfect gift that he wouldn't just buy one sweater. He would buy three, have us unwrap one, and then run downstairs and get the others—

even if we really liked the one he'd wrapped—to show us our other options. He would get so excited for us to open each gift. However, there was always more downstairs, an abundance of riches just in case something wasn't quite right. He had excellent taste, so I always loved what he picked. But he wanted to be absolutely sure he gave us the best possible gift.

I was blessed with a loving earthly father. He was not just a gift giver but also kind, compassionate, funny, and gentle. Likewise, I never had to worry about food or necessities while growing up. I realize not everyone is as lucky as I am in that regard. If you had a different experience, I hope you can still find meaning in the larger picture of this story—God's gifts to his children are so much greater than any gifts we could receive on earth. Thankfully, we all have a heavenly Father who is good in every way—so good, in fact, that he surpasses even our best definition of the word.

When I think of my earthly dad and his gifts, I am reminded of Matthew 7:11 (NIV), when Jesus asks, "Which of you, if your son asks for bread, will give him a stone?" He goes on to answer his own question, "If you, then, though you are evil, know how to give good gifts to your children, how much more will your Father in heaven give good gifts to those who ask him!"

How much more? So much more! God makes many promises in his Word to those who love him and keep his commands. He made a covenant of love with the descendants of David—a family tree which you and I have been grafted into through the blood of Jesus—that he would never fail or forsake us.

"For the mountains may depart and the hills be removed, but my steadfast love shall not depart from you, and my covenant of peace shall not be removed," says the Lord, who has compassion on you."

Isaiah 54:10 (NIV)

In his audacious love, our heavenly Father blesses "all those who wait for him" (Isaiah 30:18). God is not waiting for you to sin so he can punish you. He is longing to bless you every day of your life. **His love is audaciously abundant!** The Lord is your refuge, your strength in weakness, your light in the darkness, and your hope in times of fear. His love is greater than sin, greater even than death. He wants to unleash his blessings on you, by the power of the Holy Spirit, in the name of Jesus Christ.

REFLECT AND RESPOND

How do you best show and receive love?

_____

_____

_____

How do you show God your love for him?

_____

_____

_____

What blessings has God given you in the past year?

_____

_____

_____

What blessings do you hope to receive soon?

_____

_____

_____

Anna Henke is a copywriter/marketing assistant for the Bethany House and Chosen divisions of Baker Publishing Group. In her free time, she enjoys reading, writing, and spending time with family and friends. Anna writes about life, literature, and faith at www.annahenke.com. She lives in the Minneapolis/St. Paul area.

Pursuing

Ginger Bailey

"Your beauty and love chase after me every day of my life."

(Psalm 23:6a, The Message)

Our youngest daughter came home very sad from the neighbors' house. They had invited her on a bike ride, but she didn't know how to ride yet. But rather than giving up, the dejection she felt ignited a fire within. That night in the dark, she grabbed her bike, determined to try. She placed one foot on the pedal, moved a foot or two, and stopped. Over and over, she repeated her shaky start-and-stop motion. As she relentlessly chased her dream, her confidence grew. When she had taken flight across the safety of the grass enough times, we decided it was best she resume her efforts the next day.

In the morning when I woke up, she was already outside. She practiced a few more times on the grass and then took off on the pavement. *She took flight!* I roared in jubilation over her triumph. She rode for nearly the entire day. She couldn't stop talking about it.

Her brother, having witnessed this victory, was excited for her yet sad for himself. At nearly 9 years of age, he did not know how to ride. In fact, fear had kept him from even wanting to ride a bike with training wheels. Being on the autism spectrum and having one blind eye makes things challenging for him, especially things that require balance and depth perception. In spite of that, he had newfound inspiration.

He talked his dad into putting his sister's pink training wheels onto his bike. He outwardly convinced himself that he didn't even care that the training wheels were pink, so badly did he want to learn. As he rode that bike hard, it sparked the desire for more. Unfortunately, the small training wheels buckled under his frame. With his head hung low, he pushed the bike home. I explained that the small wheels were not meant for big kids and that we'd figure something out. I went to the place all first-world parents go for information: Google. I asked the search engine what was recommended for a child with autism. When the results said a balance bike, my heart sunk. I felt like I had failed him. *Why didn't we do that when he was little?* I wondered. But all it took was a midday text to my husband explaining the solution for him to come home after work with a solution. He had taken a bike apart and it was now stripped of its pedals, ready for my son. When he hopped on, you could tell he was excited. He would go a little and stop, get off, get back on, and go a little more. Each time he built confidence, balance, and stride. He struggled, he was frustrated, he fatigued easily, yet he kept on.

As the next few days went by, he would gain a bit of confidence, grab the two-wheel bike, try, and fail. He would take a rest, get up, and try again. Again and again, he vacillated between the balance bike and the two-wheel bike. As I watched from the window, I saw him take off from a slight incline and soar with his feet up, balancing across the driveway. *He made it!* I thought. He could balance. He must have felt it, too, because he got right off that bike, marched over to his two-wheel bike, and hopped on. I rushed out the door to cheer his efforts. He tried over and over to get his feet on those pedals. I gave him a tiny push and he took off! He came back to the grass over and over again, trying to start since he knew he could now ride. I painfully watched him fail and try again to coordinate his start. Again he took off, rode a bit, and began pedaling as fast as he could. He was free!

My son was inspired, witnessed success, wanted to taste flight, faced his fear, and overcame it! In that moment, with tears in my eyes, I heard God whisper: *That's how I chase you! That's how I want you to chase me!* His words hit me with their truth: Audacious love is pursuing. Much like my kids chased the experience of freedom when riding a bike, God chases us over and over again. He never gives up.

God took incredibly bold risks to pursue us. He gave everything he had. Like my children discovered in riding a bike, the pursuit was worth it!

REFLECT AND RESPOND

Will you do the same for God as he has already done for you? Will you courageously, valiantly, heroically, and boldly run after him? He promises that when we draw near to him, he draws near to us. In what ways is he asking you to pursue him?

_____

_____

_____

Father God, I want to live my life in reflection of how you audaciously love me. I want to run after you, chase after you, and boldly pursue you in all things. Show me by your Holy Spirit where you want me to begin.

Ginger Bailey lives with her husband and three kids in Alexandria, Minnesota. She cherishes her roles of wife, mom, business owner, worship leader, and volunteer. She's creative and loves engaging others to bring projects to completion. She's expressive in words, actions, and especially her smile, which frequently leads to conversations with total strangers.

Usable

Rhiannon Rutledge

"But Rahab the prostitute and her father's household and all who belonged to her, Joshua saved alive. And she has lived in Israel to this day, because she hid the messengers whom Joshua sent to spy out Jericho."

Joshua 6:25 (ESV)

I had just walked away from the mirror, and although makeup done, hair in an up-do, and wearing the cutest outfit I could find, I didn't like what I saw. I had lost weight, had a fresh new blue hair color, and the retro style jeans had come from the "skinny pile" that had been in the corner of my closet for years. Sure, the woman staring back at me looked pretty. However, what I felt like was a woman whose worth had been lost. A woman whose fears had taken over and begun to paralyze her. A woman who was hiding behind everything in the reflection. A woman who wasn't sure how to face the day feeling so alone, again. A woman who, through layers of pain and rejection, felt utterly unusable.

As I sat crying to be saved from the seemingly insurmountable circumstances that I had to face in yet another day, I began to hear the voice of the enemy sneak in through the cracks of my prayer time." *Your voice doesn't matter. You aren't talented enough, pretty enough or smart enough. You aren't worth the effort."*

Oh the lies the enemy tries to entangle within our hearts! We women can be incredibly talented at internalizing the enemy's lies, and we can so easily get lost in our journey to be usable by God.

In the book of Joshua chapter 2, we learn about a harlot named Rahab. That's her legacy, or at least the part of her legacy that we tend to focus on. We read the story and gloss over this woman who hid Joshua's spies, or our minds stop and judge based on a word—harlot. Yet, God saw more in her.

We read in Joshua 6 that when the wall crumbled and the armies took the city, they killed every living thing, except those in the house with the scarlet rope in the window—the house of Rahab.

Can you imagine? For six days, Rahab, who was housing her family so they could be saved as well, watched out her window as the army of Joshua marched around the walls of the city of Jericho once and left. They returned on the seventh day, and they kept marching, while anticipation grew as to what kind of destruction awaited them.

They hear the trumpets and feel the earth quake beneath them as the walls around them begin to crumble. I can imagine them sitting, huddled together as they hear the destruction of the only world they have ever known crumble around them. Rahab's faith that the spies would do as they promised and save her and her family was held by a single scarlet strand of rope.

Can you imagine how it must have felt to stand outside the fortress you had always known to be mighty and safe, now lying in ruin, its inhabitants broken and bloodied? Can you imagine seeing such destruction, while your faith in a God you have never known saves you and your entire family? I can only imagine how this must have shaped the future of this woman, Rahab, as she walked away from one life, into a new life in the promised land.

What if Rahab had believed the lies the enemy may have told her, lies that would steal from her the opportunity to be included in the lineage of Jesus.

She was a broken woman whom God saw and said, "She is usable!"

I want you to know, dear friend, that you are usable! No matter how difficult your circumstances may feel, God wants you to take what little you feel you have and leave it in his hands. He has given you a voice, and even when you feel like it can't be heard over all of the other noise that clutters the world around you, the desires of your heart are heard by Him! The gifts He has given you matter, and He wants to use you to accomplish the pieces of His story, designed specifically for you. You are usable!

There will always be difficult days. The enemy can speak loudly, using people in our sphere of influence to accomplish his tasks, but so does God. Find those around you who listen for the whispers of promise over the clamoring lies. Hold tightly to the lifeline God provides for you through them. And hold even more tightly to the promise that God has made you usable for His purposes as you journey through life.

REFLECT AND RESPOND

What lies or obstacles do you need to let go of so you can hold more tightly to the promise that God can use you?

_____

_____

_____

Is there someone in your life you can ask to come alongside you, who will remind you of the promise that God can use you?

_____

_____

_____

Rhiannon Rutledge has been married to her husband for 19 years and is a mother of three. She has a passion for writing, great red lipstick, shoes, and authenticity. She is also a children's ministry director at Five Oaks Church in Woodbury, MN.

Heroic

Kate Washleski

"Therefore, since we are surrounded by such a huge crowd of witnesses to the life of faith, let us strip off every weight that slows us down, especially the sin that so easily trips us up. And let us run with endurance the race God has set before us."

Hebrews 12:1 (NLT)

Audacious love is heroic. I know this because my husband demonstrated audacious love for me, which God used to save me from losing myself to postpartum anxiety after the birth of my second child.

My steady, anchoring husband has always been the one in our relationship with two feet on the ground, while I have a tendency to float around in the sky like a kite chasing the wind. The wind in my life before children included things like honey-do lists, adventures to experience, projects to complete. When I got excited and ran down the bunny trail, he ran with me but helped me remain realistic when I needed it, always there to pick me up when I tripped and fell down.

A beautiful example of Christ's love, I know.

Fast-forward through having a first child with special needs and the journey that led to the birth of our second baby just one week after my husband received his pastoral degree. I spent that summer home with just my baby girl, while my older one went to daycare. I navigated being a mom to a newborn much better than I remembered doing with my first, especially since I allowed myself to actually sleep when she slept most of the time.

Then I went back to work full time, just like I had done before. I'm not sure exactly when it happened, but the ugly illness and beast called postpartum anxiety moved into my body and mind and quickly tried to take over my entire life. For several months, I battled. We battled. There were moments my thoughts were so dark and my anxiety so overwhelming, I didn't know how to survive it.

My "pastor-husband" (as I now call him) walked with me through each meltdown with such grace, understanding, love, concern, and acceptance. He ministered to me as no one else could; he was there for me more than I had ever needed him to be and more than I ever thought I could need anyone. In short, he loved audaciously.

I was in therapy every other week, I went to my midwives, I tried medication. It seemed like nothing was helping. It seemed like the emergency brake on my emotional control train was broken, and when I felt overwhelmed by anxiety it seemed I had no other option than to let the train crash. It was a terrifying place to be.

Although I had been going to therapy all through the pregnancy to learn more and new coping skills to help me navigate stressful situations and anxiety, when the postpartum anxiety moved in, it felt like the illness took my tools and put them higher than I could reach. I was so frustrated. I knew the tools were there, I knew I had worked hard to gain them, and yet I couldn't access them.

My pastor-husband showed audacious love as he walked me through and helped me find tools that worked, even if it was just holding me while I bawled my eyes out and sat on the bathroom floor. He was my logical mind when the postpartum anxiety stole mine from me. He helped me think clearly when I felt clouded and overwhelmed by the illness.

The postpartum anxiety lasted about six months before I started to see the light at the end of the tunnel. We realized my body could no longer handle dairy or eggs, so I eliminated them from my diet. I started doing yoga again and writing more. The fog began to lift, and I started to do little things for myself again. The meltdowns became fewer and further between.

My pastor-husband taught me more about God and Jesus through his ministering to me, both through that season and since then, than I've learned in a long time. I experienced so much audacious love, grace, acceptance, forgiveness, encouragement, hope, and peace through my pastor-husband. His is a heroic love, minus the cape, and it pointed me to my true Hero, Jesus.

During that time, he was many times my pastor first (on call 24/7) and my husband second. He stepped up and did even more than usual with meals, kids, and household chores. When I couldn't do much because I felt so overwhelmed, he let me rest. He didn't pressure or judge me for where I was. He never made me question whether or not he was in my corner.

If you're battling mental illness, either postpartum or in general, I hope this offers you encouragement and hope as I recall all of the ways God showed up and loved me and walked with me through that season.

I pray that you have believers in your life with whom you can face the battle, so you don't feel like you're fighting alone. Jesus our Savior is the best pastor-husband that any of us could ask for, and he wants you to experience his love, acceptance, grace, mercy, healing, peace, redemption, and hope. Will you let him show you those things?

REFLECT AND RESPOND

What are you struggling with that you've been trying to handle alone?

_____

_____

_____

Who might God have in your life to help you walk through it with audacious, heroic love?

_____

_____

_____

What is God showing you as you start to name and fight your battle?

_____

_____

_____

Kate Washleski is an everyday girl trying to be intentional to follow God's leading in the opportunities she's been given. She loves connecting with people, reflecting on what she's learning, and processing out loud or in print. Kate is thankful for friends to whom it's safe to speak her mind and wear her heart on her sleeve. Read more from Kate at her blog A Wonderful Life (http://k8washleski.blogspot.com/).

Compassionate

Nancy Raatz

"When Jesus landed and saw a large crowd, he had compassion on them."

Mark 6:34 (NIV)

I heard God's call to compassion ministry but didn't believe I fit the work. I was a missionary, a mom and a wife with a degree in elementary education. I had no experience in ministry to survivors of trafficking. Surely God knew that. "Not me, God! There must be someone else." Running an aftercare home for survivors of trafficking was as far from my upbringing as could be.

I grew up in a Christian home with a firm sense of right and wrong. By high school, I had developed a severe case of self-righteousness. There were people I could hang with and people I could not. Prostituted women were among the not.

I lived my first nine years in a suburb just north of Minneapolis. A family lived a few doors down whose home I wasn't allowed to enter. I could play with their daughter in the street or at my home but was not to be in their home. As a young adult I learned the reason. The mother ran a brothel. I clearly remember being bluntly told: Mrs.

Moore* ran "the biggest whorehouse in Minneapolis." These word jarred me. I understood. They were "those kind of people."

I'm not saying my parents were wrong to restrict me from their home. The rule protected me. The problem was my belief system. I believed my Christianity didn't just make me redeemed. It made me better—superior to anyone who didn't walk as I walked. Categorizing people as good or bad came easily. Prostituted women landed in the bad category, the type of people I avoided.

And then God called me to work with trafficked women. I wrestled with God but eventually responded with a reluctant "yes." I justified my conflicted heart by embracing the idea that the trafficked woman was different, somehow more deserving, than the prostitute. In my heart, I felt the prostitute was not worthy of help. It seemed she had gotten there by her own choice, but the trafficked woman—poor thing—was tricked, robbed of her dignity, and deserved the help.

I was wrong. God's compassionate love sees no difference between the prostituted woman, the trafficked woman, and myself. I had no idea how God would use my "yes" to bring incredible change to my own heart.

In the small Eastern European country of Moldova, where my husband and I served as missionaries, Moldovan women were targeted and trafficked abroad in staggering numbers. Those who returned home were broken and unable to find healing. I remember being asked, "What is the church going to do about this problem?" And God gave me the answer. As a member of his church, I was called to respond.

We established an aftercare home for female survivors of trafficking. We built the home, planned the work, and hired staff. As I asked God how we might help women heal, he whispered that his audacious love would work through us. Eventually the joyous day came when we took in the first women.

They came broken, wounded, and ready to fight. In the first months, I saw them as women so different from myself, desperately in need of help, and to be pitied for their brokenness. My pity looked down on them and made me better than them. Surely my self-righteousness could pull them up from where life had taken them.

Then Amy came into the home with her one-year-old daughter, Nica. Amy couldn't read or write. She'd never been given the opportunity, but even if she had, the abuse she suffered early in life limited her ability. She couldn't speak a coherent sentence, and she definitely knew nothing of parenting. Amy caused my heart to break and my self-righteousness to begin melting away. Like the Grinch, my cold heart grew with love. Jesus' amazing love filled my heart and turned my pity to compassion. He allowed me to see Amy through his eyes.

She is made in his image, as am I. She is poor and without caring parents but richly his daughter, as am I. He rescued her from the bondage of a family system of evil just as he redeemed me from my bondage of self-righteousness. God filled me with loving compassion for Amy.

Compassion brings an understanding that we are all broken people, all equally in need of a savior. Compassion acknowledges that suffering breaks us all, even if we have suffered in very different ways. My self-righteous pity did nothing to help women heal. Amy didn't deserve love simply because she was a victim of trafficking but because she is a beautiful women loved by God and created in his image.

The gospels tell us that Jesus looked on people and felt compassion. Through Amy, Jesus taught me that audacious love is compassionate, and through that compassionate love, Amy chose to follow Jesus. She told a friend, "Never have I been loved like this before. I can do nothing to earn their love, but they love me, and because of this I know their Jesus is real."

*Names have been changed.

REFLECT AND RESPOND

How do you see your own brokenness?

_____

_____

_____

Where is God calling you to demonstrate his compassionate love to others?

_____

_____

_____

Nancy Raatz is an ordained minister and missionary having served in Moldova and Russia. She has a heart to see women know the joy Jesus brings. She's married to Andy and has three wonderful daughters. In her free time she enjoys cooking, walking her miniature schnauzer, and reading.

Comforting

Tabby Finton

"Surely he took up our pain and bore our suffering."

Isaiah 53:4 (NIV)

My heart felt shattered. I paced back and forth in my living room, my mind a whirlwind of questions without answers. How could this have happened? Why now? Would we all be able to endure the piercing pain of this inconceivable loss? Someone I dearly loved was suddenly gone. Tragedy had visited us again.

I wandered outside to my front porch swing and cried for hours. I remember briefly wondering what my neighbors must be thinking.

After a lingering while, I realized that I was quiet. Birds were singing. When I focused on listening, I noticed various species warbling all around. Opening my eyes brought the discovery that the sun was shining. The bright blue sky was the backdrop for the puffiest cotton ball clouds floating by. I recognized that the day was soothingly warm, with just a whisper breeze blowing my hair.

I heard children down the street laughing as they played. Somehow there was laughter in the midst of heart-wrenching pain.

Something broke open inside of me.

By no means did the situation reverse or the pain dissipate quickly.

But glimmers of hope and deep, abiding peace poked their head up through the aching to shine their light into my dark night of the soul. Love began audaciously draping its strength around me to carry me when I felt barely able to stand. The fearless, bold, and daring love of my Father God held me and sustained me through tragedy that day.

And it holds me still.

In the raw places, those difficult situations that crash into our lives so obtrusively without our permission, we can discover surprising grace. If we allow ourselves to notice, we will find that God is not far away, as our feelings often suggest. He is as close as the air that we breathe. His strength becomes our own as we linger in his presence. Allowing ourselves to rest in quietness, confidence strengthens as we consider truths from the Word. We take on fortitude and courage as we conceal ourselves for a while in the shadow of Almighty God. We can find refuge in the midst of chaos that surrounds us.

We cry out, and he hears us. He answers us with peace that goes far beyond our comprehension. Whether on the highest of heights or in the depths of despair, we find our kind Father to be faithful. Psalm 139:7-9 says it so eloquently: "I can never get away from your presence...Your hand will guide me, and your strength will support me."

But we have to choose to receive the blessings God offers even in painful situations. Accepting and receiving proffered gifts of grace, peace, strength, and courage are always our choice. We can cross our arms in defiance, declaring the unfairness of the situation. We can shake our fists in the air, shouting angry announcements to the sky. We can sputter, spout, and scream about the injustice of our plight. We can turn ourselves inward, seeing only pain instead of grace-filled remedy. And for some of us, those actions might be needed for a while, to release the agony we've bottled up inside.

We're not going to shock God with angry declarations or tantrums. He already knows and sees our hurting hearts. He just longs for us to come to him. He desires to comfort and produce in us eventual healing. He yearns to hold us close.

He will not turn us away when we come to him. Imagine Jesus kneeling down, with arms extended wide, waiting for his children to walk into his embrace. He is willing to go the extra mile to reach us where we are. Actually, He already did.

Comfort, courage, hope, and healing can be ours. In the midst of suffering, God seeks to pour in the exact remedy that will bring restoration, strength, and healing to our souls.

REFLECT AND RESPOND

What suffering have you endured that you can release to the gentle ministrations of the Holy Spirit? He wants to bring healing (and dare I say miracles?) to you today, if you will permit him.

———————————————————————————————

———————————————————————————————

———————————————————————————————

Tabby Finton is a lifelong lover of God, and she is passionate about his purposes. She's a credentialed minister and loves to speak, write, and encourage. She is mom to three sons and is married to Steve, Lead Pastor at Abundant Life Church in Blaine, Minnesota.

Generous

Becky Meyerson

"A farmer went out to plant his seed. As he scattered it across his field, some seed fell on a footpath... Other seed fell among the rocks... Other seed fell among thorns... Still other seed fell on fertile soil... This is the meaning of the parable: The seed is God's word."

Luke 8:5a, 11 (NLT)

One summer during a family vacation we visited the Museum of the Rockies (MOR) at Montana State University. It holds the country's largest collection of North American dinosaur fossils from discoveries made in and around Montana.

As we walked through the rooms filled with T. Rex specimens and met "Big Al," one of the most complete Allosaurus dinosaurs ever discovered, we came upon a group of people listening to a gentleman telling a personal story of discovery. He was a local farmer, and one spring as he was inspecting his fields prior to plowing them for spring planting, he noticed something protruding out of the dirt. Upon closer inspection, he realized this was not the usual rock or debris that works its way to the surface each spring. This was a very large bone. The researchers from MOR were called and excavated a dinosaur that had finally worked its way to the surface.

Luke 8 tells the story of a farmer who continues to plant seeds even when the soil is hardened from being walked on, filled with rocks, or weedy. This generous farmer is God and the seed he continues to faithfully plant in our lives is the Word of God.

Because of his audacious love, God has chosen to be gracious and even unconditional as he generously scatters the seed in the soil of our heart. As we meditate on God as the farmer sowing seeds in our life, our hearts should be overwhelmed with his grace and kindness. Deep in the soil of our life may lurk a dinosaur of unforgiveness, anger, disappointment, or unbelief. And bones, debris, rocks, and weeds have a way of eventually finding their way to the surface. Yet God's audacious love is generous and he never stops planting his Word in our life.

Each day, we are given an abundance of opportunities to hear God's Word through sermons, podcasts, devotionals, radio, books, live stream and more. It is a sobering thought to think that our heart may not be ready to receive the Word. Each of us know there are moments and seasons when the soil of our heart is hardened with unbelief, filled with rocks of anger, or weedy with worry and cares. Still God repeatedly scatters the seed of his Word, filled with purpose, hope, healing, freedom, encouragement, and growth. What a loving, bountiful God we serve!

REFLECT AND RESPOND

Do you have a dinosaur hidden in the soil of your heart? Can you sense that it is pushing its way to the surface?

_____

_____

_____

Do you allow weeds of worry choke out the Word of God that you hear every day?

_____

_____

_____

How can the truth of God's audacious, generous love help his Word take root so you can "produce a crop that is a hundred times as much as had been planted"? (Luke 8:8, NLT)

_____

_____

_____

Father, what a generous God you are. Thank you for the abundance of seed that you sow into my life. I invite you to come and show me the condition of the soil of my heart. I want my heart to be able to receive every Word from you and produce a harvest in my life that is a hundred-fold.

Becky Meyerson is passionate about writing and teaching from the Word of God. She is a licensed pastor, has served in churches for over 30 years and has published four devotionals. Becky is a wife, mom, and Nana. She loves to garden, try new recipes, and gather family and friends around her table. You can find her latest adventures in faith, food, and family on her website www.evergreen.study.

Present

Janae Lenning

When Jesus saw her weeping, and the Jews who had come along with her also weeping, he was deeply moved in spirit and troubled. "Where have you laid him?" he asked. "Come and see, Lord," they replied. Jesus wept. Then the Jews said, "See how he loved him!"

John 11:33-36 (NIV)

I spent my first year of college sorting through the different hurtful things I have heard from the church surrounding illness and healing. At the same time, I was dealing with chronic pain from a car accident that had happened four years earlier. What I came to realize is that yes, the love of God is manifested in his healing power, but it's also manifested in the waiting and in the pain.

The goodness and love of God are the facts upon which I continue to build my life, they're the rock to which I hold onto. Yet, in the day to day of dealing with illness, it can feel like a battle to reconcile the pain that I feel with the loving nature that we find at the core of the nature of God. Where is the room for suffering? What kind of love allows for pain, brokenness, and illness? Every action or reaction of God comes from love, so where can I find the love of God in the midst of a trial that seems unending, no matter how many doctors appointments, types of therapy, procedures, or medications I try? I have felt that the search for answers to all of my "why" questions is unending as well. This weariness has led me to start asking how and where God's love is being displayed in my given situation instead of just why. I don't know if God will ever explain to me why he acts the way he does (and I don't think he will), but I do come back again and again to find rest in the knowledge of his powerful and gentle love for us.

God's loving nature compels me to believe that the way that Jesus acts with Lazarus' sisters Mary and Martha when Lazarus has died is the way he truly feels toward those who are suffering in the world. I've often been frustrated by the way that Jesus seems to always be so willing to heal people and that he does so quickly, when oftentimes that's not people's experience. I think that's why I'm so thankful for the timing here and what's done in between:

> *When Mary reached the place where Jesus was and saw him, she fell at his feet and said, "Lord, if you had been here, my brother would not have died."*
>
> *When Jesus saw her weeping, and the Jews who had come along with her also weeping, he was deeply moved in spirit and troubled. "Where have you laid him?" he asked.*
>
> *"Come and see, Lord," they replied.*
>
> *Jesus wept.*
>
> *Then the Jews said, "See how he loved him!"*
>
> *John 11:32-36, NIV*

Jesus, the Son of God, mourns. He himself weeps with those who weep. An acknowledgement of the present reality was made by Jesus, the one who knew better than any other what the end goal would be. Jesus took time to be with those who were experiencing grief firsthand. He knew all of the platitudes, he knew how the story would end, he knew who God was in the midst of the situation, and he still wept. This is how his love was manifested that day.

This lingering presence of Jesus reassures me that the audacious love of God persists while we wait on his miracles to take place. We wonder: *What audacity must it take to risk genuine compassion by opening yourself up to suffering with your neighbor?* Yet the heart of God is unconcerned about getting hurt from entering into the painful experiences of another. Instead, in the story of Lazarus, Jesus spends time with Mary and Martha and acknowledges them in the midst of their pain. The power of presence goes beyond words. What better way to express the sentiment that "you're there for" another person than actually, physically, literally being present?

Mentally, emotionally, physically, or spiritually, we all need the presence of one another. The way Jesus models this for us shows us how love can be found in a gentle and compassionate presence which stays faithfully through the mountains and the valleys of life. Let us continue to see how God audaciously loves us through his promised presence as we seek to do the same.

REFLECT AND RESPOND

How have you seen God's love through his presence in your life?

_____

_____

_____

How have you experienced the love of another person by their presence in your life? What are practical ways that you can invest in the lives of those around you through "being there"?

_____

_____

_____

Janae Lenning is a recent Wheaton College alumni who's teaching English in France, allowing her to explore her passion for language, education, unreached people, and croissants. Chronic pain and illness struck her life at age 14, but this is only part of the picture rather than the whole story. She is passionate about real truth, laughter, and the pursuit of lasting joy.

Humbling

Nancy Holte

*"He remembered us in our weakness.
His faithful love endures forever."*

Psalm 137:23 (NLT)

Several years ago my husband, John, was diagnosed with multiple myeloma, a somewhat rare form of blood cancer. As you might guess, when you hear the word cancer it sounds loud and scary in your ears, and the thought that death could be imminent tightens itself around your heart. John was constantly tired and spent a lot of time sleeping. I remember him lying on the couch during his lunch break, trying to gather enough strength to go back and finish his afternoon of work. I looked at him with his hands folded over his stomach, still and quiet, and thought "Is this what he's going to look like lying in a coffin?" Morbid, I know, but it's hard not to go there when you're scared and weary.

From the very get-go of the cancer roller coaster, we were overwhelmed by the care, love, concern, and prayers of our friends and family. It's very humbling. And then came the afternoon when I was humbled even more by the great love of our friends. We were just about a month into the whole cancer journey, and only a few days had passed since we'd made the news public. I was going to a baby shower for a friend and her newly adopted daughter. Before leaving home, I prayed just one thing: "Lord, please don't let today be at all about me. Let all of the focus be on Jami and her beautiful baby girl."

You see, it's easy to become self-focused when walking through a tough time. Very easy. But I wanted to be able to go to Jami's shower, enjoy her baby and being with her friends, and not look like a needy person. It wasn't much to ask of God, right?

At the shower, I gladly answered people's questions when asked one on one but tried to turn the focus off our situation.

Then it happened. After she'd finished opening her gifts, sweet Jami stood up and said that before people left she'd like it if everyone would pray for John and me. She actually said that God told her not to leave before people prayed for us.

Hello?! Hadn't the Lord heard my prayer? So much for keeping the focus off our problems. Apparently he had a different plan.

I was humbled and honored and blessed beyond measure. Jami didn't know how overwhelmed I'd been. But God did, and he let me know that he saw me, loved me, and would take care of me. I don't understand how or why God urges people to pray for others. It seems to me that if he knows someone needs prayer, he could just, you know, tell himself. But I've decided that maybe God nudges us to pray for others so that we get to be part of the miracle. What amazing love, huh?

I was so encouraged and humbled by Jami's friends (many of whom were also my friends) when they prayed for us, but mostly I felt like God had bent down from heaven and placed a little kiss right on my forehead.

"As soon as I pray, you answer me;
you encourage me by giving me strength."

Psalm 138:3 (NLT)

I'm happy to say that we made it through that challenging season of our lives. God held us every step of the way, and my husband is in remission to this day. Praise be to the God who heals!

REFLECT AND RESPOND

Have you ever felt a God kiss? May I encourage you today to write it down? It's so easy to forget and yet it's an amazing faith builder when you go back and read about it years later.

_____

_____

_____

Spend a few minutes talking to God about who he'd like you to pray for today. After praying, consider reaching out to that person with an encouraging text or phone call and let them know you prayed for them today.

_____

_____

_____

Nancy Holte not only loves to laugh but considers it a critical part of human survival. If you were to ask, most days she'd say her glass is half full. When it starts reaching the half-empty level, Nancy looks for a funny book or movie, knowing that indeed, laughter is the best medicine. Nancy is a speaker and freelance writer, encouraging women to embrace all that God has for them. You can connect with her at www.nancyholte.com.

Our Shame

Susie Larson

"And I am certain that God, who began the good work within you, will continue his work until it is finally finished on the day when Christ Jesus returns."

Philippians 1:6 (NLT)

The other day, my son Jake called to chat. Even during his wandering years, he called regularly to sort through his questions and concerns. This particular day he struggled to understand why it's so difficult for him to receive generous gifts from others.

We revisited an experience from his teenage years. Though typically reliable and obedient, he made a costly choice one winter night.

Long story short, he pulled into a parking lot, spun around in the snow, hit a concrete structure, and caused about three thousand dollars' worth of damage to my truck. He was devastated. I was stunned.

We sat down as a family and processed what happened. Jake's little brothers asked him questions and he humbly answered them. Kevin leaned in with fatherly strength and said, "Son, you've just taken a huge withdrawal from the 'trust' account. We have to deal with the consequences of this costly choice. However, I want you to know something: Your account is not empty. We love you. We still trust you and respect you. You are a trustworthy son."

Now I sat on the edge of my treadmill and held the phone close to my ear. "Jake, do you remember what you were doing when Dad said those words to you?"

He whispered, "Um, no. I don't."

I continued, "You gripped the arms of the chair and looked down at your feet. You couldn't even look up at him."

Jake went silent on the other end.

"Honey? Are you there?"

His voice cracked. He whispered, "Mom, I always knew you and Dad handled that incident brilliantly, but I couldn't exactly remember how it all played out that day. Something got in me when I made a choice that so defied the things I care about most. I could never imagine that I'd do what I did. I've never really been able to get past it. Oddly, I had no idea that my posture was so shut down when Dad spoke to me. I faintly remember his words now, but they sure didn't go in back then."

"That's shame, son. That's what got in you that day. It's shame. Could it be that underneath your strong work ethic is a heart that doesn't believe that God might want to lavish a goodness on you that goes beyond your efforts or even beyond what you think you deserve?" My voice cracked as I asked such probing questions.

Again, more silence from Jake.

Then, my big, husky, first-born son started to cry. I sucked in a sob.

"Oh, honey. Can I just tell you? I love you so much. And that shame? It's not from God and it's not from us."

We both struggled to find words.

He then asked me, "Is this what has held me back all these years? Is this why it's difficult for me to receive out-of-the-ordinary kinds of gifts? And why I don't ask for your help or for God's? Because of shame?"

"I think so, honey. But imagine how delightful your relationship with God could be if you learned to approach and even pursue him with assurance and confidence, convinced that he's good and that he has set his affections upon you. I'd say, right now, you're missing the best parts of this relationship. But what joy for you to discover an unhindered, joy-filled relationship with your Father who loves you and loves to lavish his goodness upon you! Doing so will affect every aspect of your life: your work, your play, your bike riding, and your morning coffee with your wife."

After my conversation with Jake, I wondered:

Is shame just a negative emotion and a skewed mind-set, or an actual parasitic force that drains life, takes life, and keeps us from the life God has always intended for us?

Consider what's true about some of the mind-sets we often embrace:

- It's not humility that compels us to shy away from God and ask little from him—it's shame.

- It's not integrity that keeps us from asking for God's help when we need it—it's pride, independence, and shame.

- It's not noble to go without something that God has promised to provide—it's an orphan-mentality rooted in shame.

- It is not justice that keeps us far from God after we've blown it— it's shame.

- It's not kindness that keeps us from "bothering" God with our persistent requests—it's either spiritual laziness or shame.

We don't have to try and convince God to be good to us. In fact, he's the one trying to convince us to receive and walk in his goodness.

Here's what's true for the person who is in Christ, and is therefore, his joint-heir:

- We are recognized in the heavenly court and have every right to appear before the King, assured of his glad welcome. (See Ephesians 3:12; Hebrews 4:16)

- We have an Advocate—Jesus himself. He intercedes for us day and night. We're not bending the ear of an unrighteous judge in effort to get his attention. (See 1 John 2:1; Hebrews 7:25.)

- We have the affection and attention of our star-breathing God who loves us and intends to finish what he started in us (See Psalm 18:6; Philippians 1:6.)

I used to think of being shameless in only negative terms: someone with no social awareness or sense of common decorum, someone with no fear of God and no concern for others.

And while that alarming aspect of our culture is growing by leaps and bounds, let's not throw out its counterpart: Shameless—audacious, unconcealed, undisguised, transparent, unashamed.

Jesus invites us into his presence without shame, without our past baggage, without the need to cover ourselves or to be someone we're not, without the enemy's constant taunts in our ear telling us we're not enough, and without the self-deprecating slurs we constantly hurl at ourselves.

Jesus wants us invites us into his presence, expectant and full of faith—full and free, healed and whole.

REFLECT AND RESPOND

How often does shame keep us from audaciously running into the arms of our Father not only to receive grace just after we've blown it, but to dare to ask for things we could never earn, deserve, or acquire on our own?

_____

_____

_____

Adapted from Susie Larson's book, Your Powerful Prayers (Bethany House Publishers, 2016).

Susie Larson is a radio host, author and national speaker. She hosts her own daily live talk show, *Live the Promise with Susie Larson*, which airs across the Upper Midwest and in several other locations around the country. Active in local ministry, she is the author of 12 books, including *Your Beautiful Purpose* and *Blessings for the Morning*. Susie and her husband, Kevin, have three adult sons and three amazing daughters-in-law and live near Minneapolis, Minnesota. Learn more at www.SusieLarson.com.

My Fear

Dawn Zimmerman

"So we keep on praying for you, asking our God to enable you to live a life worthy of his call. May he give you the power to accomplish all the good things your faith prompts you to do."

2 Thessalonians 1:11 (NLT)

I was about to walk on stage to accept an award before an audience of accomplished business leaders and I could hardly breathe. I stood in a bathroom stall outside of a grand ballroom pleading with God.

My heart was racing. All I could think about was my seventh grade Student Council speech when I hyperventilated. As a somewhat shy but strong-minded teen, I tried to piece together the sentences I had rehearsed. All that came out were really loud donkey sounds. The student body erupted with laughter. As my embarrassment grew, so did the volume and depth of the "hee haws." I can laugh about it now, but it was horrifying at the time.

The emotion of that day rushed over me in that bathroom stall. I prayed and prayed that God's presence would take over and I would not recreate that 13-year-old memory at age 26—now with a bigger platform and what felt like even more to lose.

Thankfully, God showed up that day (and I didn't). I stepped up on that stage with notes in hand and never looked back at them. Many business leaders I had never met came up to me afterward to tell me how well done the speech was and how it moved them. I smiled and thought, "If they only knew." God took my weakest moment and turned it into something only he could.

Less than a year later, public speaking became a part of my work, and I now speak in front of groups regularly. Most people would never imagine the anxiety I felt before taking the stage and how it crippled my speech once I did.

We can look like we have it together even when we don't. I lean on God—constantly—to give me direction, confidence, and perseverance through my fears and challenges. I know God can equip and he won't let me fall, at least without a good reason.

I used to think that following my purpose centered only around my strengths, that God used me when I had the steps figured out and the skills to execute. But he has taught me that it is in my time of weakness—when I feel like I cannot do it alone—that I step aside and let God take center stage. Whenever fear rears its head inside me, it's a signal to me to invite God on the journey.

I no longer push my weaknesses aside or run from opportunities that scare me because they lead me to rely more on God and to focus on my purpose in this world.

God designed each of us for a unique purpose, and he uses both our gifts and weaknesses to refine us and shine through us. I've learned it's not about a course of action, but rather a cause of action. It's less about where I am going and more about why I am going there. It's all about God.

I later learned that donkeys developed their loud "hee haw" noises to keep in contact with their family. I never imagined that calling out to my Heavenly Father would sound like that. But I love it. God has a sense of humor, too.

He took me from wounded donkey to professional speaker. It's a purpose I never expected. That's not to say the fears are gone. They actually are why I continue to speak often. They make me turn to God, rely on him, and remind myself of my desire to live a life worthy of his call—not mine.

It's in those moments that I recite Paul's words to the Thessalonians (from 2 Thess. 1:11) in my mind: "So we keep on praying for you, asking our God to enable you to live a life worthy of his call. May he give you the power to accomplish all the good things your faith prompts you to do."

I could easily feel like I don't measure up. But it's not about me. It's about God, and he most certainly measures up. Before I take a stage, I still need to pray diligently that God's presence will overcome me. I no longer fear that I will hyperventilate. But I definitely still need God to take over and let my words reflect him.

I want to live a life worthy of his call—no matter the embarrassment, insecurities, or challenges that may arise. They provide an opportunity for me to step back and God to step forward so the spotlight is on him

REFLECT AND RESPOND

Where are you letting fear or your feeling of weakness hold you back?

_____

_____

_____

How can you pursue the purpose God has designed for you this year?

_____

_____

_____

Dawn Zimmerman is a writer, speaker, and communications coach. She founded The Write Advantage on the belief that everyone has a story to tell. She is the mother of two life-giving kids and falls more in love with her husband each year. She's a lover of words, lakes, adventures, and the unexpected.

My Comfort Zone

Julie Fisk

"'You must love the Lord your God with all your heart, all your soul, and all your mind.' This is the first and greatest commandment. A second is equally important: 'Love your neighbor as yourself.' The entire law and all the demands of the prophets are based on these two commandments."

Matthew 22:36-40 (NLT)

"Mom, I'm making it for Emma."

Examining the swirls of color covering her daughter's art project, my friend paused at these words, knowing that Emma had, through cruel words and actions, made her daughter cry during their bus rides to school. But she watched as her daughter continued painting, creating a 7-year old's masterpiece for a girl who had repeatedly bullied her.

My friend slowly swallowed the objections that immediately came to mind and intentionally decided to let events unfold, praying silently over the painting, over her daughter, and over Emma.

A week later, her daughter danced up the driveway after school, delighted and breathless as she told my friend that Emma loved the gift, having proudly told another child that it was a gift from a *friend*.

Her daughter had turned an enemy into a friend with a painting of butterflies.

It turns out that a seven-year-old is braver, more audacious than me when it comes to extending grace and love to someone who hurt her.

And the result of her audacious love was God-breathed: the healing of someone else, the closing of a chasm, peace.

As I work (continually) through what it truly means to put my inward faith into outward actions, the story of the Good Samaritan is the gold standard to which I strive.

You see, Jews walked miles out of their way to avoid walking through Samaria because to be a Samaritan was to be an enemy, a person you did not associate with under any circumstances. And yet it was the Samaritan, not the priest nor the community leader, who intentionally moved toward the injured stranger lying on the side of the road instead of skirting him with averted eyes (Luke 10:31-33). It was the Samaritan who scooped him up, bandaged him, and paid for his room, promising to return and pay the balance of his stay and care (Luke 10:34-35). It was *the enemy* who was the example of a true "neighbor" in Jesus' parable (Luke 10:29-37).

This is audacious love. And it is as far out of my comfort zone as anything I've yet to encounter.

It's easy to love those who are loveable, those who look like us, those who follow the same rules and cultural norms as us. Being loving and kind to our friends is not our measuring stick. In fact, Luke 6:32-33 reminds us that even unrepentant sinners do this.

Instead, let us be Samaritans, people who care enough, love enough to cross all the man-made boundaries to care for others who might not, if the roles were reversed, do the same for us. Let us set aside fear and be both bold and gentle, loving audaciously outside our comfort zones, asking Jesus to order our steps and set forth our path, trusting him to change lives and this entire world, one brave, audacious "yes" at a time.

REFLECT AND RESPOND

Reread the story of the good Samaritan in Luke 10 with the understanding that the Samaritan was culturally considered an enemy by the audience to which Jesus spoke. Prayerfully consider what this new understanding of this famous parable means for you in your own faith walk.

Prayerfully consider how might you be acting like the priest or the Levite in the parable, either intentionally or unintentionally.

Who might Jesus be calling you to love audaciously this week? Begin including this person in your prayers, and perform one act of kindness toward him or her this week.

_____

_____

_____

Julie Fisk is passionate about encouraging women in their individual faith journeys. She is the co-author of several books, including *The One Year Acts of Kindness Devotional* (Tyndale, 2017). Julie loves adventuring with her children, coffee with girlfriends, and quiet evenings with her hubs on their backyard patio. You can find Julie at www.theruthexperience.com.

My Circumstances

Grace Kasper

"Trust in the Lord with all your heart,
And do not lean on your own understanding.
In all your ways acknowledge Him,
And He will make your paths straight."

Proverbs 3:5-6 (NASB)

"I'm sorry." I told him through tears. "I can't."

I pulled the ring from my finger, set it on his desk, and left.

Some things can seem very murky when you're in the midst of them. That's how I frame that season of my life.

Looking back, I thought it was love. Extreme weight loss, migraines, and the worried faces of family and friends told me it wasn't. Though we'd met at church and shared common theology, our relationship was not healthy. Many of our interactions were driven by my fear and his control. As my clothing and personality changed, the dynamics only got worse.

I found a defense or rationale for everything that was happening, thinking that hiding the issues was honoring him and guarding our relationship. I explained things away to my friends, to my family . . . even to myself. I didn't want to admit that I had been wrong to say yes to him. I didn't know how to explain that you could love someone and yet be afraid of him.

For a long time, I'd been wrestling with questions and doubts.

Trying to quell them with the same refrain… *I can't find a Scripture to back up my concerns. We have the same theology. I'm a sinner too, so I can't judge his heart. Lord, give me a sign.*

Maybe he'll change.

I had a known future. I knew where this would lead—children, a brand-new church plant, and an eventual cross-country move. *Maybe this is what God has for me.* And yet I was so unsettled internally that I couldn't move forward. It wasn't until the abuse became sexual that God gave me a wake-up call and the strength to leave. Just a short time before we were to be married, I gave back the ring. With a heavy heart—but one finally at peace—I walked away from what was known. I walked away from a pending marriage, a tight-knit church community, and a man who was choosing to build a life with me.

Have you been in this position? Sometimes we, like Abram, are called from a known land to a land unknown, trusting only in the love of our Father. These steps of faith can lead us to give up financial security, a city we love, or a soon-to-be marriage. But our painful decision to obey him will bear more fruit than any earthly comfort.

There are seasons when God will tug at your heart and redirect your steps. Saying yes in that moment can ONLY happen when we're assured of God's audacious love for us. The same God who gave up his son for you calls you to walk with him through every season. It may mean a season of prolonged singleness. I spent a long season pursuing my own healing and growth after calling off my engagement, unsure if I would ever marry. When God finally did bring my husband into my life, it was better than anything I could have hoped for.

Today, remember that God's radical, audacious love is greater than your fear of the unknown. It's greater than the gossip you may face for taking that step of faith. It's greater than the whispers of those who don't fully understand your actions or think your decision was foolish. God's love will shield you and give you the strength to face an unknown future. His love is greater than marriage, the perfect job, or well-behaved children. Lean on his love and let the peace come in.

REFLECT AND RESPOND

How has God's audacious love given you peace in the midst of heartache?

_____

_____

_____

What stands in the way of your full surrender to God?

_____

_____

_____

Grace Kasper loves the thrill of storytelling through media. She was blessed to do this working alongside Susie Larson on her national radio program _Live The Promise with Susie Larson._ Currently she works with Baker Publishing Group, helping authors find creative ways to share their own stories. Grace and her husband, Rob, live in St. Paul with their 9-lb. Chihuahua, Romir.

My Safety

Sue Donaldson

"Christ sacrificed his life's blood to set us free, which means that our sins are now forgiven."

Ephesians 1:7 (CEV)

On June 28, 2016, four ISIS suicide bombers attacked the Istanbul International Airport. As I watched the television news that evening, I saw a video clip replayed over and over of panicked people, desperately stampeding away as fast as possible. Then I noticed one man—an official, judging from his white uniform—who ran the opposite way: directly into the crowd, not away from it. He could've been killed, yet he kept running into the fray. Frantically waving his arms, he beckoned everyone to follow his lead. I could almost hear his words: "Come here! This way! This is the way to safety!"

And they followed him.

I thought, *That's what audacious love does.*

Audacious love goes toward danger to bring another out of danger.

Audacious love risks self to save another's life.

Audacious love gives no thought for personal safety, only for the care and protection of others.

Christ loved audaciously.

When I saw that man in white, I thought of Christ. But I also thought of me.

Could I be like that man? Would I run into the crowd, not away from it—no matter the risk or sacrifice, no matter the embarrassment, inconvenience, or time involved? For the sake of another's real, eternal life?

Would I be like that man?

God calls us to audacious love through the ministry of reconciliation, leading people into right relationship with him.

In 2 Corinthians 5:19-20 (ESV), Paul wrote, ". . . in Christ God was reconciling the world to himself . . . entrusting to us the message of reconciliation. Therefore, we are ambassadors for Christ, God making his appeal through us."

Wow. To live a life through which God makes his very appeal—an appeal for reconciliation.

Sometimes I wish he didn't trust me that much. I don't view myself as particularly courageous. I'm not sure why he included me, but I do know that you and I are entrusted with that message.

Recently a young man who is close to our family came to visit our home for a couple nights. We love him. We know him. But he doesn't believe there is a God.

I remember praying. *Lord, make me a minister of reconciliation for Brendan. I want to run right into his doubt and fears and bravado and wave him the way to safety. Show me how. Give me courage. Help me show your audacious love. Amen.*

We talked about God that visit and the next. I made Christ's appeal by making his favorite drink (decaf, no cream) and preparing his favorite breakfast (pancakes with blueberries *and* chocolate chips.) I spoke life-giving words. I served in Christ's name, by his power, for his sake; small attempts to clear the way to the cross. I didn't do it perfectly. I wasn't as brave as that man in white. I didn't exactly risk my life.

Next time I want to do better, ask God for more courage, to live and love audaciously.

Lord, make it so. May I love as you did, one life for another's. Waving my arms, if necessary.

REFLECT AND RESPOND

Are you willing to be the one who runs into the fray of those who are desperately looking for life and safety in God's arms?

_____

_____

_____

In what ways can you prepare yourself now to be ready to respond to the needs of others rather than focusing first on personal safety?

_____

_____

_____

Will you pray that prayer with me? _Lord, help me live so you can make your appeal through my life. Thank you for entrusting me with the ministry of reconciliation. May I love bravely, authentically, audaciously—one life for another's. Lord, make it so . . . necessary. Amen._

Sue Moore Donaldson speaks and writes to introduce God's welcoming heart—inviting you to know the Ultimate Host and pass on his invitation. She and her husband Mark live on the central coast of California and have raised three semi-adult daughters (which means she's always at the bank or on her knees.) Sue blogs at http://welcomeheart.com/sue-donaldson, and is a frequent speaker for women's events. You may view her speaking topics at http://welcomeheart.com/speaking.

My Abilities

Kristin Demery

"Only let each person lead the life that the Lord has assigned to him, and to which God has called him . . ."

1 Corinthians 7:17 (ESV)

There have been several times in my life when I've failed. There was the driver's test where my temporary paralysis in the face of an oncoming ambulance, sirens blaring as it raced down the middle lane where I was located, was acidly described by my tester as "the icing on the cake of my failure." There was the time my infant niece accidentally rolled off the tall, king-size bed when I was babysitting, landing with a hard thunk on the floor. And then there was the time when I—again, accidentally—started my microwave on fire.

There have also been times when I may not have been an outright failure but still felt like one. Case in point: I love to write, but I'm a terrible reporter. Working in silence with just my laptop for company is one thing, but cold-calling someone who may or may not want to talk to me? That always took an hour of psyching myself up and more deep breaths than I care to remember.

During my years working in the newsroom, I mainly worked as a copy editor, a role that is behind-the-scenes in nature and right up my introverted alley. But since my hours were part time, I also took on odd jobs, writing on a wide variety of topics.

But of all of the things I wrote about, the stories that made the most impact on me were part of a series on inspiring women. There was the woman who overcame horrendous abuse from family members and strangers to become an advocate for women experiencing domestic abuse. There was the woman who helped cancer patients cope with chemotherapy by gifting them with gorgeous wigs and hats. There was the woman with a passion for helping abused and neglected animals find new homes.

Whenever I had conversations with these women over the phone, it's wasn't unusual for the story to resonate so deeply that I'd find myself in tears.

Yet even though it seemed clear to me that these women were indeed exceptional, what continued to fascinate me was the way in which, without exception, these extraordinary women thought they were ordinary. They hesitated over the word "inspiring." Even though their names had been brought to my attention through others, rather than through their own efforts, they felt unworthy.

And yet, wasn't that true for me, too? I was the one writing the stories, yet I felt ill-equipped. Other reporters could think up better questions. Surely someone else was wittier, smarter, or more knowledgeable. In an attempt to combat my own insecurities, I found myself mimicking those who seemed to do it so well. I tried to write with the same attention to detail and depth of emotion that Amy did. I tried to make my voice sound smooth and unperturbed on the phone like Kirsti did. And I suppressed the parts of me that quailed every time I had to pick up the phone.

I think as Christians, and perhaps more so as women, that feeling of inadequacy is something we're all too familiar with combatting. We deflect compliments or downplay our own efforts. We think in terms of how we could do or be better. And we never, ever feel like we're doing it "right."

That struggle is real, and yet God's audacious love calls us to live a life of confidence—not because of anything we've done but because of our identity in him. Recently, a friend reminded me of this truth:

God doesn't call the equipped, he equips the called. That sounds like a pithy mantra, yet it's a sentiment that is echoed throughout the Bible. 2 Timothy 1:9 (ESV) says, "[Jesus] saved us and called us to a holy calling, not because of our works but because of his own purpose and grace, which he gave us in Christ Jesus before the ages began."

Did you notice the timing? The calling comes first. It's not predicated by our skills or our knowledge, our life experience or talents. No, our calling is something that God places within us, something God-ordained and God-breathed and worthy of a holy confidence.

I love the way The Message says it:

> *"But you are the ones chosen by God, chosen for the high calling of priestly work, chosen to be a holy people, God's instruments to do his work and speak out for him, to tell others of the night-and-day difference he made for you—from nothing to something, from rejected to accepted."*

> *1 Peter 2:9-10*

You're accepted and loved and, most of all, worthy. Don't let your fear of failure drive you to mimic others or accept less than God's best for you. Instead, trust in God's audacious love for you and his purpose for your life.

REFLECT AND RESPOND

What's your calling?

_____

_____

_____

Ephesians 4:1b says, "…I urge you to live a life worthy of the calling you have received." Do you struggle to feel equipped in your calling? Why or why not? If so, how can you gain confidence through knowing God's love for you and his purpose for your life?

_____

_____

_____

Kristin Demery is married to her best friend, Tim, and is a mom to three girls. Her background in journalism has led to many roles, from managing a social networking site for moms to working as an editorial assistant for an academic journal. She is the co-author of several books, including _The One Year of Daily Acts of Kindness_ (Tyndale, 2017). Find more from Kristin at www.theruthexperience.com.

Me

Jennifer Veilleux

"Well-behaved women seldom make history."

– Laurel Thatcher Ulrich

It was a sea of pink, pointy hats and witticisms on fluorescent poster board. The January sky in Minnesota was bullet gray, but the temperature hovered around a balmy forty degrees, and no lumps of white snow impeded the marchers as they streamed along Summit Avenue on their way to the capitol. The day after the inauguration of the forty-fifth president of the United States, millions gathered around the world to nonviolently raise a collective voice under the banner of human rights.

As I watched the throngs of people go by, sometimes laughing, sometimes chanting, constantly taking selfies and sending Snapchats, I felt the rumble of the thousands of feet and the bass from the speakers set up on the capitol lawn and the brisk winter wind go right through me. With spasms of hope and grief alternately shooting down my spine, this was as close as I'd ever come to touching audacity. This was what it meant to be part of something that was larger than myself. Despite our differences, that day it seemed we were all in agreement that what united us was greater than what divided us.

No matter what side of the spectrum you fall on when it comes to hot-button issues or politics or religion, it takes boldness to stand for what you believe in, to stand when you've been kicked down, and to stand for the rights of someone else. It takes courage to plant yourself like a rock in the middle of the stream, to claim a voice when you've long been told that you didn't have one or it didn't matter.

Feminist and womanist biblical scholars such as Elisabeth Schussler Fiorenza, Kristina LaCelle-Peterson, Wil Gafney, Nyasha Junior, and others have long been pointing to the bold temerity women displayed in the Bible. These women who would do anything for the love of a child, for the love of community, for the love of their God—the only one who they knew would see them, listen to them, and help them. They were those who defied cultural convention because they saw in God a savior who was willing to do the same.

I will give the child I've waited for my entire life over to the service of God (1 Samuel 1:22).

I will hide the spies in Jericho, even though it might cost me my life (Joshua 2:4).

I will be a servant of God and trust that God will do the miraculous (Luke 1:38).

I will live my entire life in the temple until I see the newborn Jesus (Luke 2:36-38).

I will touch the cloak of his garment and be healed, even if it means revealing my illness to the crowd (Mark 5:25-34).

I will sit and listen, though societal gender roles tell me it's not my place (Luke 10:39).

I will believe that Jesus can raise my brother from the dead, even though I am angry and grieving (John 11: 21-24).

I will ask for healing for my demon-possessed child, even if our people are enemies (Matthew 15: 22-28).

I will wash Jesus' feet, even if I am belittled, shamed, and cast aside by men (Luke 7:36-50).

I will dedicate my life to Jesus after he casts out my demons (Luke 8:2).

I will choose to believe in life after death, even if those around me sit in locked rooms in fear (John 20:1).

I will respond when Jesus calls my name (John 20:16).

***

Nine months from that cold January morning, I boldly made my way down Summit Avenue once again, this time alongside thousands of others running the Twin Cities Marathon. This time when I rounded the bend toward the capitol, I almost wept to see the finish line before me, anxious to rest my weary body but also overcome with accomplishment. While we are a long way from the eternal finish line, when we march and we race together, we come ever closer to the audacious love of God.

> "Here's to strong women. May we know them.
> May we be them. May we raise them."

> *–Anonymous*

REFLECT AND RESPOND

What women in the Bible do you most identify with? Who do you least identify with? Why?

_____

_____

_____

What other examples of women acting audaciously can you find in the Bible? What do you think it meant for them to act that way?

_____

_____

_____

Jennifer Veilleux puts commas in books by day and fights fires by night. A graduate of Western Carolina University and Luther Seminary, she lives and works in Bloomington, Minnesota. You can find her doing burpees at her local Crossfit every morning at 5:30.

My Self-Image

Amy Green

"So he got up and went to his father. But while he was still a long way off, his father saw him and was filled with compassion for him; he ran to his son, threw his arms around him and kissed him. The son said to him, 'Father, I have sinned against heaven and against you. I am no longer worthy to be called your son.'"

Luke 15:20-21 (NIV)

The volunteers in the aisle handed us small colorful slips of paper before the closing praise song. From the front, the worship leader explained, "We want you to write down a prayer request anonymously. We'll collect the papers and redistribute them so you have a chance to pray for a brother or sister."

What a great example of community, I thought as I wrote down something real but impersonal—a sick relative, I think. I heard the scratch of pencils around me and assumed everyone else was doing the same thing. "Please pray for safety for my family's travel." "My friend is struggling with an important choice." "I need patience for a situation at work." Things like that.

Once the prayer requests were collected and handed back out, I took a folded green slip of paper. There, in messy penciled block letters were three words: "Am I worthy?"

I stared at the words and realized that every person in the room was secretly asking that question. It was the unwritten prayer request of every heart…and a kind of theological trick question, because there are two wrong ways to answer it.

1. No, I am a worthless failure who God probably hates…if he notices me at all.

2. Yes, of course I'm worthy. Look at all the good things I've done!

Both untrue based on what we know from the Bible, but oh so familiar. Have you heard them recently? The whisper of condemnation that you'll never be good enough, that you're a failure as a wife or mother, that no one could ever love you? Or the whisper of approval that you're an example to others, that you have a right to be proud of what you've accomplished, that God must love you better than others?

They're the same lies believed by the prodigal and the older brother from Jesus' parable—one whose shame kept him from returning home and one whose pride kept him farther away from his father's love even though he never left home.

But there are two right ways to answer the question "Am I worthy?"

1. No, we aren't worthy because we can't earn our salvation and deserve death for our daily rebellion and sin. The moments when we think we've got it together, that we're above temptation, and it's those other people out there who are unworthy of grace, we're in for a fall.

2. Yes, we are worthy because Christ's death on the cross reconciled us to God. We will one day approach the throne of God with confidence, not fear of judgment, because in Christ we are holy and blameless and able to stand.

But even that isn't the full answer. Fast forward to the end of time, when all nagging questions will be answered and all fears and failures removed. The songs in Revelation we'll sing around that throne aren't about us and whether or not we're worthy. They're a beautiful, unending loop of God's complete worthiness and everything he deserves—power and wealth and wisdom and strength and honor and glory and praise.

I kept that green paper in my pocket for years until I felt God leading me to pass it—and the story—on to someone else. A reminder, folded and tucked deep inside, that the Father always welcomes us home.

Because, sisters, the final answer to the question isn't yes or no, or even both. When we ask if we're worthy, God answers with his audacious love: "I am worthy. And you are mine."

REFLECT AND RESPOND

Do you tend to struggle more with shame (fearing you're unworthy) or pride (believing you're worthy on your own)?

_____

_____

_____

What truth from God's word can you use to replace the lie about where your identity is found?

_____

_____

_____

Amy Green is an enthusiastic youth group leader, homemade bread baker, and hard-question asker who lives in Minneapolis, Minnesota. She blogs about life, faith, and pop culture once a week at themondayheretic.wordpress.com.

The Lies We Believe

Crystal Dill

"The thief's purpose is to steal and kill and destroy.
My purpose is to give them a rich and satisfying life."

John 10:10 (NLT)

As I sat in my room one day, I suddenly became overwhelmed with sadness and weeping. Ordinarily I was a typical teenage girl, happy and easygoing, but that day the cold dark atmosphere of my bedroom mimicked the state of my heart. I began to have thoughts of self-hatred and self-injury. I felt the urge to take the screwdriver lying on my nightstand and carve the word "HATE" on my hand. As I tearfully began to scratch the back of my hand, a shift in the atmosphere came over me, and I felt love enter the room. I knew I shouldn't be doing this. The love that came in intruded on the darkness that surrounded my thoughts. It was almost as if I heard God, with his audacious love, say, "Pick up your Bible." Although I had grown up in a Catholic home, I had never opened the Bible that I received from confirmation the year before. But at that moment, feeling hope in my heart, I opened the cover.

Selecting a page at random, I opened to Psalm 138: "In the day when I cried out, You answered me, and made me bold with strength in my soul…Though the Lord is on high, yet He regards the lowly.. Though I walk in the midst of trouble, you will revive me; You will stretch out your hand against the wrath of my enemies and Your right hand will save me. The Lord will perfect that which concerns me; Your mercy, O Lord endures forever; do not forsake the works of Your hands."

It was the first time I heard God's voice. I felt like he was speaking right to me, that he saw me and would rescue me. It was the first time I trusted that *God's love was greater* than any darkness I could face.

So often we can feel powerless, defeated, or hopeless when circumstances weigh on us. Even worse, we accept the lies Satan throws at us as a "cultural norm." Yet when we read scripture, we are told that we are not of this world, that we are set apart because greater is he that is in us! My prayer is that God will continue to embolden us to rise up and say no to the lies of the enemy and yes to God's greater love.

Luke 10:19 says, "I give you the authority . . . over all the power of the enemy and nothing shall by any means hurt you." What Luke means is that we are counted victorious through Christ—and that we can combat anything God has not ordained for our lives. Jesus wants us to take up the authority he sacrificed for us to have. The enemy would love nothing more than for us to settle in this life, lay down our spiritual armor and lose this great battle. But we know the truth: The enemy has been overcome "by The Blood of The Lamb and the word of their testimony" (Revelation 12:11).

Knowing that, we can speak God's Word over our lives and wield our weapons of war. His word is "sharper than any two edged sword" (Hebrews 4:12).

The world tries to convince us that it's perfectly normal and even heroic to resign ourselves to the things that bind us. We are even *admired* for admitting we have issues and trying to handle them on our own, but we cannot allow ourselves to drink in this lie laced with truth.

What is *truly* empowering is embracing the freedom Christ brings, saying no to the enemy and yes to God's great love. As patient, trusting warriors, we know the hope that we have in Jesus, the one who makes us "truly free indeed" (John 8:36).

Through the years, I've learned that the dark thoughts I once had toward myself were not part of God's purpose for me. Since then, I've learned to grab tightly to my Savior's hand as I arm myself with his truths and the freedom they bring.

REFLECT AND RESPOND

Is there an area in your life in which God and his great love do not seem greater than what you face?

_____

_____

_____

What truths from God's Word can you stand on right now?

_____

_____

_____

Crystal Dill is married to her own personal comedian, James, and mom to her creative 9-year-old son, Lincoln. She finds joy in sharing life and coffee with other ladies who have a hunger for God and watching them rise from a struggling faith to a vibrant relationship with Christ. Besides family game nights and outdoor adventures with their foxy-dog, Red, she enjoys journaling and blogging her journey with Christ. You can connect with Crystal at doubletakerise.wordpress.com.

My Loneliness

Patnacia Goodman

"I've told you these things for a purpose:
that my joy might be your joy,
and your joy wholly mature."

John 15:11 (MSG)

"I'm so sorry, but I don't think I should keep seeing you."
I have a fairly active imagination, but I never imagined getting broken up with in a parking garage. Yet there we were. Honestly, I wasn't that surprised. I'd felt it coming, and I knew it was the right call. He was a good guy and we'd had a good time together, but it just wasn't right. We parted amicably, and the case was closed.

Yet two weeks later, I still couldn't shake the thought of him and everything we could have been. As I lay in bed one night, feeling more irritated than sad, the root of my discontentment struck me suddenly as a singular thought seared my mind.

I'm lonely. I'm stuck because I'm lonely.

Little by little the pieces started coming together, revealing motives I'd been ignoring for far too long. Loneliness had led me to seek attention and validation wherever I could, whether it was through rekindling friendships or pursuing new relationships. In this case, the discontentment prompted me to look for a distraction, and the one I picked was about six feet tall and had the kindest eyes. At the time I didn't recognize what I was doing, but lying in bed that night, it became clear to me that I had been using him, and now that he was gone the loneliness was back in full force.

Soft laughter mixed with tears as I absorbed the simple revelation that night. Staring at my dark ceiling, I whispered to the only one I knew would hear me, "Lord, I see it now. I'm lonely. How pitiful is that?"

Almost instantly, John 15:5 rolled into my mind and calmed my thoughts.

"I am the Vine; you are the branches. He who abides in Me, and I in him, bears much fruit, for apart from me you can do nothing," (NKJV).

Abide. Abide in me.

I had moved away from my true Source, the love and strength of the Lord, and planted myself in the garden of approval-seeking. It worked for a little while, too. I was connecting with people, building relationships, and feeling pretty good about myself while doing it. The thing is, attention and approval could not sustain me, and the moment I felt disconnected from those around me, whether through their rejection or my own lack of effort, the well of approval demonstrated just how shallow it stood.

Abiding in Jesus is a choice, a choice we make and prove by selflessly showing others the love of God and keeping his commands. And it is a choice that comes with a wonderful promise:

> "These things I have spoken to you, that My joy may remain in you, and that your joy may be full."
>
> *John 15:11 (NKJV).*

Joy is a sure remedy to loneliness and rejection. Joy forces our eyes off our circumstances because it isn't based on our circumstances. It's a reaction to the outpouring of the audacious love of God. It's a wonderful gift we access when we abide in the Lord, which is the only way to experience true joy.

My friend, I've experienced loneliness and lived in the dullness it brings long enough to say this with absolute certainty: Only a pure and mature joy makes real satisfaction possible during a season of loneliness. In fact, when I am connected to the all-encompassing love of Christ, I feel an inexplicable joy that makes it easy to be alone without feeling lonely. Instead of seeking out my friends to fill a void, I can reach out to them out of a genuine desire to be with them. I can go to a coffee shop alone without feeling self-conscious. I don't need to look for validation in relationships because I am tapped into my true Source—the Vine.

He is the Vine. What a gift from the Author of true love, who can turn our tears of loneliness into joy-filled laughter.

REFLECT AND RESPOND

Have you ever let the joy of the Lord overshadow a difficult situation you were facing?

_____

_____

_____

How can you stay connected to Christ as the True Vine?

_____

_____

_____

Patnacia Goodman is a word-loving, winter-hating Minnesota native. She is living her high school dreams, working for Bethany House and Chosen Books as an acquisitions assistant. She loves coffee shop-hopping, playing board games, and occasionally updating her personal blog. For more musings and ramblings, find her at patnacia.wordpress.com or on Instagram @patnaciag.

Our Ugliness

Sarah Kallies

"Therefore, since we are surrounded by such a great cloud of witnesses, let us throw off everything that hinders and the sin that so easily entangles. And let us run with perseverance the race marked for us, fixing our eyes on Jesus, the pioneer and perfecter of faith."

Hebrews 12:1 (NIV)

Picture Mary Magdalene in your mind. What do you see? Now hold on to that image because we will come back to it.

King David, Simon Peter, the apostle Paul, and Mary Magdalene. All are famous Bible characters. We know them well. They have been ingrained in the teachings of the church. Each of them now commands a place of honor and respect to the believing world. They were special: selected by God, by Jesus, to play leading roles in the story of the world.

And with such notable roles, there comes a weight. A responsibility. To know each person for the specific purpose that each of them was chosen. To understand and honor what God intended for his glory through their lives.

David was a man after God's own heart. Peter was the first disciple chosen. Paul was the founder of the Church as we know it. Mary was the first to see Jesus after the resurrection.

But what happens when you attach the favor of God and fame with a single fallible human being?

All too often, we rewrite history. We cloud the truth with what feels good, with what's convenient to us and our culture. We live in a culture that encourages half-truths and impossible standards. As a result, we put our biblical heroes on a pedestal, stripping away the bits of information that taint their storylines. Because if God chose them, they must be incredibly good. Right?

Wrong.

I think that these particular people are perfect example of the unreasonable love of God. His grace. His mercy. His Sovereign ability to love us at our most broken. To not just love us, but to use us—because of our weaknesses, not in spite of them. To see our failings and love us directly in the middle of the mess we have made of our lives. Unconditionally.

Because the truth is that David, Peter, Paul, and Mary Magdalene had something remarkable in common. They were broken. They all had overwhelming sin in their lives at some point. In fact, if they were alive today they would be considered the scourge of society, all deserving of severe judgment and discipline. We would reject them on sight. David was an adulterer and murderer. Peter denied and betrayed Christ at the most critical point possible. Paul was a genocidal maniac. And Mary Magdalene? Prostitute. Adulterer. Demon-possessed. Those are just a few of the tags she has received over time.

Not exactly the cream of the crop.

But every movie, picture, or portrayal of Mary Magdalene I have ever encountered has her playing the role of a Hollywood heroine. She is gorgeous: Long hair, great body, face of an angel. But honestly, how likely is this? In my experience, not very.

As a mentally ill, recovering addict and alcoholic, I have been to rehab. I have lived with and gotten to know women who are actual Marys. The mentally ill. The call girls. The AIDS-riddled.

The reality is that almost all of them fall in the category our current culture has deemed as worthless, even ugly. Both in character and physical appearance. These women, myself included, are scarred addicts missing teeth. Diseased in different ways. Borderline suicidal.

I think Mary Magdalene was probably one of us. One of the shattered ones. Just a nothing life of bad decisions and regret. And suffering for it.

Now picture Mary again. How does what Mary really looked like stack up against how she has been portrayed?

It is not until Jesus comes into the picture that things get interesting. Because it's this indescribable love that only a Father, a Savior, has for his children that can see past horrifying mistakes and into the heart of a person. The place where our purpose and calling has always been predetermined, regardless of what we have done.

The love and grace of Jesus does not focus or hold on to our flaws. Instead, this audacious love seeks out every opportunity to take those very failings and use them to usher in the Kingdom of God right here on earth. To take what was meant for harm and make it beautiful.

If God used these damaged people in Scripture to teach us for eternity, imagine what he could do with you, right now. Wherever you are in your walk.

How incredible that we serve a God that longs for us to lower our guard. To be transparent. To identify the areas where we struggle and then give them over for him to use. For our sin to be turned into a weapon in the arsenal of heaven.

Hebrews 12:1 (NIV) says, "Therefore, since we are surrounded by such a great cloud of witnesses, let us throw off everything that hinders and the sin that so easily entangles. And let us run with perseverance the race marked for us, fixing our eyes on Jesus, the pioneer and perfecter of faith."

Make the choice to allow what was meant to hinder you and watch it be turned into something beautiful because you have chosen to fix your eyes on Jesus and not the things of this world.

REFLECT AND RESPOND

Where are your eyes fixed today? Is there a sin or issue, past or present, that has you entangled and is hindering you from moving forward?

_____

_____

_____

Consider God's audacious love for you, flaws and all. How can you choose, today, to let him turn the "ugly" moments in your past or present into something beautiful?

_____

_____

_____

Sarah Kallies is a Minneapolis-based speaker, author, singer, mother, wife, mental illness fighter, assault survivor, and most of all, intense lover of Jesus. Her work can be found on her website at sarahkallies.com, Facebook, Instagram, iTunes, and Twitter.

Step Out

Amber Gerstmann

*"Let your love, God, shape my life with salvation, exactly
as you promised; Then I'll be able to stand up to mockery
because I trusted your Word. Don't ever deprive me of truth,
not ever—your commandments are what I depend on.
Oh, I'll guard with my life what you've revealed to me, guard
it now, guard it ever; And I'll stride freely through wide open
spaces as I look for your truth and your wisdom; Then I'll tell
the world what I find,
speak out boldly in public, unembarrassed.
I cherish your commandments—oh, how I love them!—
relishing every fragment of your counsel."*

Psalm 119:41-48 (MSG)

H ere I was for the umpteenth time in front of an audience of whom
I was scared to death. It was almost my moment to step into the
spotlight, and my lips were bleeding. No one could tell; I chewed
them inside my mouth as I fretted away my anxieties. *Will I remember
the words? Will this be impressive enough?* Why *did I agree to do this? I
want to go hide in a dark corner.*

I had terrible performance anxiety, that dark corner of my mind
suffocating me in fear, causing me to avoid any bold moves because
they just might be the wrong ones or, even worse, be met by
disapproval.

I'm not exactly sure where it started, but somewhere along the way I picked up this awful idea that the world had purchased tickets to the performance of my life and held up low-numbered score cards to each thing they saw. And I figured God did, too. I pictured life with Jesus as more of a tightrope walk than anything even remotely spacious. At any moment I could say something unkind, act with the wrong motive, or pass up an opportunity to shine my light and find myself falling headlong off the tightrope of his approval.

So in that dark corner of anxiety I hid, not making any sudden moves.

I don't know about you, but to me the *stride* is reserved for the tall. Long, lean supermodel-type legs (probably, I'm sure of it) traipsing, frolicking freely wherever they go with a perpetual catwalk and slow, almost angelic arm swings. If I had supermodel legs I would traipse, too. But let's be real, when my non-supermodel five-foot three-inch frame is doing a *stride,* it may as well be the "Prancercize." ("What's that?" you say? Google it. You're welcome.)

But as silly as it might sound, that is how I picture the carefree steps Psalm 119 speaks of, "...and I'll stride freely through wide open spaces. . . ." That space is so welcoming, so generous, so *safe.* And so opposite the way I lived.

I'll never forget the moment this truth first shined its light into my anxious hiding space. "What are you doing over there?" Jesus asked. So kind, so unassuming, arms extended in invitation to something greater. He spoke his great love for me and the security of his grace, not dependent on my behavior or performance, dependent only on him. He reminded me, "I have come that you may have life and have it more abundantly (John 10:10 *ESV*)," and that no height or depth or a long list of other things could separate me from his love. Wide open space indeed.

This extravagant, audacious love changed everything for me. Not only did I realize this space was safe to live and move in, I also learned it was safe to rely on his Spirit within me. His voice guides my life, steers my heart, and, above everything else, speaks love. Every time I feel that familiar tightness of anxiety, Jesus whispers, "It's a wide open space. You're safe in the next step and the next after that, even in front of people. I've got you. I love you."

God's invitation into the wide open calls to each of us, and I'm starting to believe it is the place of our greatest effectiveness. Here we are not trying to protect ourselves in anonymity or some vain pursuit of perfection but are instead trusting Jesus to shield, guide, and use us for his glory.

So here's where I stand, and I want to invite you into this same freedom. The incredible, audacious love of Jesus offers us a wide open, abundantly free life with him. He'll change us where we need changing. He'll guide us where we need guiding. And perhaps best of all, he'll invite us into adventure with him to discover purpose for our life. He's already got a plan.

So come on out of whatever dark corner you've been hiding. Step out into the wide open. There you'll find me in stride, no longer afraid. And maybe, just maybe, doing the Prancercize.

REFLECT AND RESPOND

In what areas of life do you feel unprotected or afraid to take the next step?

_____

_____

_____

What is one way you can step into your purpose in the wide open space of God's love and grace today?

_____

_____

_____

Amber Gerstmann is wife to Trevor and mom to three little wiggles. She's a minister, worship leader, Bible/theology teacher, and total coffee snob. Amber is passionate about communicating the great love and truth of Jesus, and when she's not chasing her littles, one can typically find her dabbling in photography, running, or singing.

Love When It's Hard

Sandy McKeown

"Do to others as you would have them do to you. If you love those who love you, what credit is that to you? Even sinners love those who love them. And if you do good to those who are good to you, what credit is that to you? Even sinners do that."

Luke 6:31-33 (NIV)

I don't remember exactly what I said, but I know I shouldn't have said it: I sassed my mother.

We were almost home, so she hurriedly drove in and parked near the farmhouse. With dust swirling about the car, she was around the opposite side faster than I knew she could move. She yanked me out of the back seat, slamming the door shut, and began ramming my head repeatedly into the side of the car. As she did, she roared her reasons why I was wrong to sass her. I was approximately 11 years old at the time.

My older brother heard what was happening while doing chores in the barn and came running, waving his arms, yelling: "Stop it! Stop it! Stop it!"

She turned to argue with him, and as I stood there, watching the two of them scream at each other, a thought dawned: *She's not supposed to be doing this!*

How easy is it to do good to—and love—someone who has hurt you?

Jesus was beaten and scarred. Those who were closest to him denied having a relationship with him. Yet, he loved them. He loved those who persecuted him. The heart of the Son of Man did not respond according to how people treated him. He loved them no matter what they had done.

Discovering my mother had been abused herself was a beginning, and I eventually learned to forgive her. Then I recognized that, because she had never worked past her hurts, her emotional growth had stagnated. She was incapable of having the mother/daughter relationship with me that I desired.

I had hoped for a mother I could share my dreams and struggles with, who would model for me how to do life.

She was not capable. She didn't know how.

When we were together, we talked about the latest recipes she had discovered. We talked about her daytime "soaps." Later, when she entered a nursing home, we watched her favorite TV reruns from the seventies and played endless rounds of cards. They were the activities she enjoyed.

In Mom's final years I traveled often to spend the day with her. Due to shortage of personnel at the home, I would assist in her care as needed. My brother asked, "How can you do what you are doing for her?" My answer was simple: because I forgave her.

I couldn't wait to love my mother until she asked for forgiveness. Her self-awareness hadn't reached that capability. I couldn't wait until she was ready to have the relationship with me that *I* wanted. She didn't know how.

I had to find a way to love her just as she was, with all her flaws.

Last year for Mother's Day I wasn't able to drive the two hours to see Mom because I was speaking that weekend. I apologized and promised to call her the day after. She was especially cognitive that morning, more than usual, and we talked and laughed for over an hour. The laundry staff had lost one of her favorite bras and she had asked repeatedly for it to be returned to no avail. We discussed, with great laughter, the possibility of her wheeling her chair to the intercom at the nurses station and announcing for all to hear: "I want my bra back!"

When I got off the phone with her that morning, I reflected on how much fun we'd had. It was a gift, I knew. What I didn't know at the time was that a month later she would be gone.

I had learned to love someone who didn't love me as I wanted to be loved; I had learned to put aside the hurts and disappointments and come to realize she loved me in her way.

Years ago, I stopped wishing for a relationship that could never be. This year, I mourn the relationship we eventually found. I had wanted a mom that would teach me how to do life better. I think she did. She taught me how to love the hard to love.

REFLECT AND RESPOND

Who in your life is hard to love?

_____

_____

_____

What good can you do for that person today?

_____

_____

_____

Sandy McKeown and her husband are the parents of five children, three with extra challenges. Sandy uses life experience combined with powerful insight and creative humor to convey true hope to all audiences. You can contact her at sandymckeown. com.

Rest

Jen Spiegel

"Are you tired? Worn out? Burned out on religion? Come to me. Get away with me and you'll recover your life. I'll show you how to take a real rest."

Matthew 11:28 (MSG)

The day I realized I was depressed wasn't at all what I would have expected. It was a beautiful June day, and I was fresh off a weekend retreat with some of my favorite people. I should have arrived home happy, energized, even relieved that the retreat project I'd been working on for months had been a huge success. But standing at the kitchen sink, I stared down into the drain and let it wash over me for the first time.

I didn't feel refreshed or accomplished. I felt mind-numb exhausted and soul-numb sad.

Part of me had hoped this weekend away was going to be what "fixed" me. Leading up to the retreat, I knew I was tired. And I knew the degree to which I was pushing myself was hurting me physically. So I cut a few stressful things out of my schedule. But this little getaway—time away from home and daily responsibilities, loving and serving others—felt like the perfect recipe for overcoming the "blues" that had been dogging me for months.

Arriving at the retreat, I decided I needed to get busy if I was going to kick this thing. I spent the next three days chasing what I felt I'd lost, searching for my old self, trying whatever I thought might help me ditch the perpetual chill that had settled just under my skin.

Lists. Maybe I need more lists. There's just so much to do. So I wrote tasks down and crossed them off, trying to stay one step ahead of the darkness.

Hugs. I like hugs. Maybe I just need more hugs. So I pulled friends close and grasped for warmth.

Naps. Yes, I'm sure a nap is just the thing. So I cozied up to my pillow and stared at the wall, telling myself I'd feel better if I could just turn it all off for a few minutes.

But back at home, as I plucked a runaway blueberry out of the sink drain, I realized none of it had worked.

I couldn't outrun, out-hug, or out-nap this thing.

I needed to rest.

I had been working myself into the ground, inadvertently slipping into a pattern of fighting for God's favor, feeling the need to prove myself over and over again.

Psalm 103:11 (CEV) says, "How great is God's love for all who worship him? Greater than the distance between heaven and earth."

Likewise, Romans 8:39 (NLT) says, "Nothing in all creation will ever be able to separate us from the love of God."

And 1,600 years ago, St. Augustine wrote, "God loves each of us as if there were only one of us."

We humans certainly have reason to be confident in God's love. But we have never been able to wrap our minds around this concept for long. Instead, we've spent our entire history trying to prove our worth.

Is there anything more audacious, or more difficult, than believing God's love for us isn't tied to anything we do?

Depression can make a person feel very small, like they're shrinking. I get it now, that feeling of little pieces of yourself dropping off here and there—pieces you've come to depend on. During a difficult moment, you look for your right hand—your usual optimism, patience, tenacity—and find it gone.

But in a world that screams for more and bigger and better things, maybe one of the most audacious moves we can make is to become small—to stop chasing greatness and start bending low, stop trying to climb higher and start realizing a mountaintop was never the goal.

So I began.

I audaciously folded laundry and cleaned peanut butter off sticky little fingers, and I remembered that a good life is made mostly of being grateful and graceful in the seemingly endless tiny moments.

I audaciously sat on the deck with a good book and a big glass of water, and I learned that sunshine, hydration, and a story with a happy ending are great medicine.

I audaciously felt my big scary feelings and began listening to my body, addressing the physical aspect of my situation.

I audaciously looked for a big God in small places—in my sink full of dirty dishes, on my yoga mat, between my tomato plants—and I found him there, holding out the little pieces of me that had dropped off.

And I continue to audaciously forgive myself when I fall, when I fail at it all a million times, when the darkness creeps close.

I nestle into a Big Brave Love that says it's okay to be small.

It's okay to be broken.

It's okay to rest.

Because there's no way to earn what has already been given.

REFLECT AND RESPOND

Have you ever found yourself chasing approval from God or other people? Where did it lead you?

_____

_____

_____

Recall a time you felt small or maybe even broken. Read Psalm 103:11-18. How does an understanding of God's audacious love affect your outlook on challenging situations to come? How might it impact your future goals and plans?

_____

_____

_____

What is one way you can "be small" today to remind yourself of God's no-strings-attached love?

_____

_____

_____

Jen Spiegel is an advisor and editor for Bridging the Gap's writing team, where she shares her passion for honest storytelling and helping women discover the healing power of writing. She enjoys date nights, outdoor adventures with her family, and curling up with a good book and a one-eyed dog named Finn. You can connect with her through her blog, www.storiesinthetrees.com.

See Beyond the Hurt

Kandy Noles Stevens

"I will instruct you and teach you in the way you should go;
I will counsel you with my loving eye on you."

Psalm 32:8 (NIV)

As long as I can remember, I have wanted to be a teacher. The "future career" line in my Dr. Seuss *My Book About Me* copy includes just one word, "TEACHER," etched in my best first grade penmanship. Little did I know that much of my education on becoming a great teacher would come from answered prayers and the bad boys of the seventh grade.

As a first year teacher, I wanted to share my passion for learning and inspire young minds. No one ever prepared me for the students who didn't love learning or who were facing more challenges than I had ever experienced. Any teacher who says they simply adore every one of their students is either stretching the truth or, as my grandmother would say, "hitting the sauce."

Many kids are hurting in this world, and inevitably that hurt spews out. One group of junior high boys I taught often acted like a fourth grade volcano experiment. Hurting children don't have one stereotypical look, but I did discover one universal truth about their lives and stories. Inappropriate behaviors are often a manifestation of an unmet need. It is hard to teach someone who is starving, desperately needs a hug, or desires for someone to believe in them.

Some days were battles of wills, others filled with pure exhaustion. Many times I wanted to walk out the doors and never look back. It was one of those days when I finally did exactly the thing I should have done all along. I asked God to help me see these precious students through his eyes.

What a game changer! One morning I relayed to my class how my family and I had gotten lost in the woods after dark the previous Friday. When I explained that it wasn't the best family night we'd ever had, my students were riveted. My heart, however, wasn't prepared for what happened next. For years after sharing this story, one after another, the students who had been seen as "problems" before asked me what my plans were for family night.

I learned that if I asked God for a correction in my vision, I needed to be prepared to have my heart broken in the process. My heart stung as each of those kiddos confessed that they really wished to have time with their family.

I suddenly realized that God didn't just want me to teach science and math. He wanted me to open my heart to love my students through their broken places, their struggles in learning and life.

Soon after this epiphany came a colossal struggle with one of my strongest-willed students. After a series of disruptions, it looked like the classroom wasn't going to be big enough for both of us. With every act of willful disobedience, he reached closer to my last nerve. Just before I lost my temper, God gently reminded me to love fearlessly. I walked over to his desk, got down on my knees, and quietly explained that I had a contract outlining my responsibility to teach all the students in my class and that he was preventing me from living up to those expectations. I assured him I really wanted him to stay, but if he couldn't do that, I would trust his judgement on what to do next. His perplexed look said, *You aren't going to yell at me and send me to the principal?* I assured him I believed in him and really hoped he would stay. His perplexed and repeated inquiries of "Are you kicking me out?" were met every time with steadfast love. The whole episode ended with him staying in the class and finishing that day's assignment flawlessly.

It was a turning point in my career. God showed me how loving his children audaciously was more important than any other lesson I had planned for the day. In reality, I will never be able to teach anyone anything unless they know how deeply I care for them first. And I have an answered prayer and group of seventh grade boys to thank for being a better educator to all the students who followed them.

It's been almost twenty years since God used a young man to teach me that if I love students boldly, there is nothing stopping them from reaching the stars. We don't run into each other often, but when we do, I still get the biggest hugs from him and a quiet thank you for not giving up on him.

REFLECT AND RESPOND

Is there someone in your life you find challenging to love?

_____

_____

_____

Could the hurts they carry be placing a wall between your love and their needs? If so, ask God to help you see others through his eyes.

_____

Consider one way you can reach out to that person this week with a demonstration of audacious love.

_____

_____

Kandy Noles Stevens describes herself as a science teacher by day and superhero (mom, doctoral student, and community volunteer) by night. True to her southern roots, Kandy has a story about everything, which she often shares on her blog, www. kandynolesstevens.com. Her first book, _The Redbird Sings the Song of Hope: and Other Stories of Love Through Loss_, was published in 2016, and showcases Kandy's down-home style of writing which leaves readers in tears, fits of laughter, or better yet, both.

Serve Others

Kendra Roehl

"So now I am giving you
a new commandment:
Love each other.
Just as I have loved you,
you should love each other."

John 13:34 (NLT)

"This is silly, I don't even know what I'm doing."
I berated myself as I sat in a parking lot with an empty truck I had planned to fill up with donations that never came. I thought of the vehicles I'd arranged to pick up clothes from a local business—another flop, or at least it seemed that way. I wondered once again if I was up to the task ahead of me.

Several months earlier I'd agreed to take over the Diva Boutique, a shop set up at a Single Moms Retreat for women to come and gather free clothing and accessories donated by other individuals and churches throughout the year.

Lord, I am not a clothes person. Everything nice I own I've gotten from my sister! I'm completely inept in this area. Couldn't you have found someone better suited and more talented to take on this role?

I waited. But no response came.

As I made the hour long trip back to my house, I prayed and

determined once again that I would finish this project that I believed God had asked me to do—even if it killed me.

And through this process I learned something amazing about God.

Although my vehicle hadn't miraculously filled up with clothes on my way home that night, little by little, day by day, God began to bring things to us. A bag of clothes from a neighbor, a moms' group who brought jewelry, a church that collected at their women's event. Every day more and more would come. And as we did the hard work, putting in countless hours to sort and fold and pack, we realized God had indeed provided.

I spent the months leading up to the event sorting through the donations we received, keeping only the highest-quality pieces, wanting the women to know they were cared for, even in the smallest of details.

After bringing everything to the camp to set up for the weekend, we had lunch with Carol, the organizer and director of the retreat, and she told us stories of the women who'd come the first year, stories of God's provision, love, and acceptance. Then she told us how excited she was for the coming year, anticipating that God would again show up in incredible ways.

Her excitement was contagious, and as we finished setting up the boutique, we took a moment to pray. We prayed for the women who would come. We prayed blessing over their families and lives. We prayed that God would meet them at the retreat, that they would sense his love, even in the smallest of ways.

And then we waited. Excited to see what would happen, knowing we'd done our part. We'd planned and prepared. We'd worked. Now the rest was up to God.

As the women began to trickle and then slowly flood into the boutique, we saw needs being met all over the room. One woman cried upon finding the winter coat she'd been praying for. It fit perfectly. Another woman needed a dress for her daughter's wedding in a very specific color, and it was there, in her size.

There were tears and whispers of "How could you know I wanted this?!" all over the room, over and over and over again. The simple answer was, "We didn't, but God did."

As I thought back to those months leading up to the retreat, how little by little God brought the donations to us, knowing exactly what we needed, what the women desired, I was in awe.

Only God could do that.

As I watched women find things they not only needed but also simply wanted, I thought, *God loves to bless his children. He cares about the smallest of things. Things we wouldn't even think of asking for because they seem so insignificant.*

And yet, to a loving father, they are not. I watched God bless his daughters that weekend. I saw God's audacious love extended in ways I would have never imagined.

REFLECT AND RESPOND

When have you seen God's audacious love extended to you in a way you didn't expect?

_____

_____

_____

In what small ways can you now extend that same love by serving others around you?

_____

_____

_____

Kendra Roehl is a wife, mom, author and speaker. She's written four books, including _The One Year Daily Acts of Kindness Devotional_ (Tyndale, 2017). You can find her writing honestly about life, motherhood, social justice, and kindness at www.theruthexperience.com.

Keep Fighting

Karah Hawkinson

"Blessed is the one who perseveres under trial because, having stood the test, that person will receive the crown of life that the Lord has promised to those who love him."

James 1:12 (NIV)

I will never forget the day I stood in my dermatologist's office after a month of being covered in an itchy rash. The doctor's assistant gave me a sympathetic look and said, "I don't know how you put up with it." *As if I have a choice?* I thought. Reminding myself that prison orange is not a good color on me, I settled for giving her a mom glare that could have melted steel.

But I learned an important lesson through that experience. We don't get to choose which battles we'll have to face in life. In some cases there truly is no such thing as giving up.

In my case, that was literal. I couldn't take off my itchy skin and walk away. My father-in-law can't say, "I give up. I don't want to have cancer anymore." My friend at church can't say, "I think I'm going to be done having a special needs child." We can't bring back the dead. Sometimes we just have to accept that this is the life we lead and get busy fighting.

In other situations, we may have the option to walk away, but choosing not to keep fighting comes with a cost. You can leave a difficult marriage, but you can't keep your family intact. You can give up on the dream of going back to school, but you can't have the dream job that requires that degree. You can stop going through painful medical treatments, but you may be giving up the possibility of healing.

When we give up on a challenge that will eventually lead us to good things—a battle we know we should be fighting—just because the process is difficult to bear, we walk away from hope.

I don't know what challenges you're facing today. They could be physical ailments, broken relationships, sin struggles, financial hardships—anything that makes you wish you could give up. But as long as there is a fight, there is hope. God's audacious love gives us the strength to keep fighting, keep trying, and keep finding hope.

Deuteronomy 31:6 (NIV) says, "Be strong and courageous. Do not be afraid or terrified because of them [your enemies], for the Lord your God goes with you; he will never leave you nor forsake you." The battle is hard. It hurts, and it's exhausting. But you are never alone. God is with you no matter what. Deuteronomy 31:8 continues, "The Lord himself goes before you and will be with you; he will never leave you nor forsake you. Do not be afraid; do not be discouraged."

This reminder was so important that Moses repeated it. God will never leave you. In fact, he's leading the way down your difficult path.

In Romans 8:38-39, the Apostle Paul writes, "For I am convinced that neither death nor life, neither angels nor demons, neither the present nor the future, nor any powers, neither height nor depth, no anything else in all creation, will be able to separate us from the love of God that is in Christ Jesus our Lord."

Take a minute and personalize that verse:

For I am convinced that neither _____ *nor*
_____ *(list as many as you need!) will be able to*
separate _____ *(your name) from the love of God that*
is in Christ Jesus our Lord.

Write it down and read it often to remind yourself that no challenge you face can separate you from God's audacious love. He is FOR you, and he's right there with you, fighting on your behalf and giving you the strength you need to bear your burdens and fight your seemingly impossible battles.

REFLECT AND RESPOND

In what areas of your life have you given up the fight?

_____

_____

_____

What has that cost you?

_____

_____

_____

What can you do to get back in the battle, realizing that God will never leave you nor forsake you and that he fights your battles alongside you?

_____

_____

_____

Karah Hawkinson is a wife, mother, and professional historian from Coon Rapids, Minnesota. Her passion is global hunger relief, and she uses blogging, publications, and social media to help average Christians make a positive, lasting impact for the world's hungry. Follow her guilt-free, hope-filled blog at www.foodshelffriday.com.

Empower Others

Kelly Radi

*"Therefore encourage one another
and build one another up, just as you are doing."*

1 Thessalonians 5:11 (ESV)

"Stop it . . . now!" she snapped through clenched teeth. "If you two don't quit this minute, we're going home without lunch." The hungry baby in the navy blue sling gurgled and began to fuss as the other two children—a boy and a girl—continued to bicker and prod, their screeching voices noticeable in the restaurant during the already-crowded lunchtime rush.

Sitting at a table just a few feet away were three women of a "certain age" out to enjoy a nice quiet lunch and some friendly conversation. The chaos at the next table escalated and several people in the area began to stare, their unspoken words of disapproval clearly evident. The young mother, teetering on the edge of exhaustion and tears, was trying to discreetly breastfeed the infant and wrangle the toddlers when their tray of food arrived. The hungry children grabbed at their plates, splattering a full glass of milk across the floor and onto the designer handbag of one of the ladies. That's the moment when all three of the women turned to face her. Fully expecting scowls and a reprimand, the mom was shocked to look up and see their warm, compassionate smiles.

"Oh, dear, we've all been there," one said. "We promise it gets easier."

The second chimed in, "In fact, we used to bring our kids here, too. Now they're all grown up and we only wish they had time to join us for lunch. As tough as it is in this moment, try to savor the time you have with these cuties. They are precious gifts from God."

The third woman spoke softly to the wide-eyed children, telling them how lucky they were to have a mom who loved them so much and who took them on grown-up lunch dates. Then she went to get a refill for the spilled milk.

Instead of berating the young mother, these women built her up! They chose to give her grace and shower her with loving words of encouragement. What effect do you think these gentle comments had on the young family? Do you think they impacted the remainder of the meal? How about the rest of the afternoon? Do you think the young mom went home defeated? Or do you think she went home feeling like she could tackle another day as a mom of three children under the age of four?

This is one example of how we, as Christian women, can empower one another—how we can humbly reflect his abundant, audacious love through our actions and our words in everyday life. This is the kind of love that Jesus demonstrated (and continues to pour over us) time and time again. It's powerful. It's inspiring. It's life-giving. It's the kind of love our Savior calls each of us to extend to our fellow mothers, wives, sisters, grandmothers, coworkers, friends, and even strangers. We are to "encourage one another and build one another up."

Imagine the change in our world if every woman chose to respond with smiles instead of scowls. Support instead of judgment. Kindness instead of condemnation. What if our default was simply love? How awesome to pass this legacy on to future generations! Our families and workplaces would thrive. Our churches and communities would flourish. Today, I challenge you to make a difference and spread his audacious love, one smile and one spilled glass of milk at a time.

REFLECT AND RESPOND

What can you do this week to give grace and offer encouragement to somebody who needs it? Do you have a friend, coworker, or family member who could use your gift of loving support? The next time you're out in public, seek opportunities to share his audacious, abundant love!

_____

_____

_____

Kelly Radi is an award-winning author and speaker who has a special place in her heart for women. She's not afraid to share her less-than-perfect-but-always-authentic experiences in hopes of empowering others. Her book, *Out To Sea: A Parents' Survival Guide to the Freshman Voyage,* is a resource for parents as they navigate the high school-to-college transition.

Receive Love

Kristen Ostrem

"Yet to all who did receive him, to those who believed in his name, he gave the right to become children of God. . . ."

John 1:12 (NIV)

One evening, I was meeting a friend for dinner. As we neared the café counter to place our order, I secretly contemplated paying for both meals. My friend spoke up before I did, however, and offered to pay for my food.

"And pick out a coffee drink, too!" she added.

As someone who rarely buys coffee drinks for myself, to now spend this person's money on an unnecessary drink felt somewhat uncomfortable. However, I felt God prompting me to receive the gift graciously.

I ordered my food and beverage, then turned to my friend and said, "Thank you!"

She looked at me and responded, "Thank you for receiving that."

In hearing her remark, I was taken aback by the entire occurrence, as it exemplified a lesson God was trying to teach me: to receive his love. During this brief interaction, God asked me to receive my friend's gift, and when I did, he verbally thanked me—through my friend's mouth—for doing so.

You see, although I grew up in church, my mind's default belief for many years was that God's love was somewhat obligatory and performance-based.

In my early twenties, hoping to sound humble, I prayed: "God, you don't have to show or convince me you love me. I know (in my mind) that you do. I am okay with just being your vessel and showing other people you love them."

But since that time, God has taken me on a journey of understanding his actual, limitless love in a deeper, more personal way. One of God's greatest lessons came when I felt him speak a concept to my heart—that I need to allow him to show me he loves me. If I don't let him show me his love, I am actually rejecting him, because he *is* love. (1 John 4:8)

Since my dinner-date revelation, I have been practicing a lifestyle of receiving the love God wants to demonstrate. Over the years, he has continued to show me his audacious love in countless ways: through incredible grace, needed friendships, random surprises, answered prayers, timely or encouraging words, provision, and by rearranging my schedule so I can rest and spend time with him.

I do not believe for a second that God is a genie in the sky nor someone whose benefits we should seek more than knowing him. Yet his Word says he is the rewarder of those who diligently seek him, that every good gift comes from him, and that he is love.

Unlike my wrong thinking and naive prayer, God's love isn't conditional, limited, or a trick, but rather, it is decided, available, and without measure.

My prayer is now, "God, give me everything you have for me today, and give me grace to see and audaciously receive you."

REFLECT AND RESPOND

Have you ever struggled with knowing or believing God's love? If so, ask God or consider asking a mentor to help identify what the untrue belief might be: unworthiness, performance-standards, shame, or other. What biblical truth can you meditate on to oppose this false belief?

_____

_____

_____

Have you ever considered receiving God's love as a necessary component for knowing Him more fully? In what ways can you receive God's expressions of love today?

_____

_____

_____

Made in the USA
Monee, IL
20 September 2021